NEWS
that is
GOOD

Evangelization for Catholics

NEWS
that is
GOOD

ROBERT J. HATER
Preface by Alvin A. Illig, C.S.P.

AVE MARIA PRESS   Notre Dame, Indiana 46556

Father Robert Hater is a professor of Religious Studies at the University of Dayton. He also does pastoral work and resides in a Cincinnati parish. He is a former associate pastor, high school teacher, and director of religious education of the Cincinnati Archdiocese. Father Hater holds his doctorate from St. John's University in New York and is the author of a number of articles and books including *Holy Family: Christian Families in a Changing World* (Tabor), and *Parish Catechetical Ministry* (Benziger).

Sections of the following chapters first appeared in the following publications: Chapter 5, "Catholic Evangelization: Word, Worship and Service," in *Catholic Evangelization in the United States of America*, January/February, 1988; Chapter 6, "Evangelization and Conversion," in the article "Facilitating Conversion Processes," by Robert J. Hater in *Christian Adulthood: A Catechetical Resource*, copyright 1987, USCC, Washington, D.C.; Chapter 8, "Evangelization and Fundamentalism," in *Church*, National Pastoral Life Center, Winter, 1988.

Some material appeared in *Holy Family* by Robert J. Hater, published by Tabor Publishing, Allen, Texas, and in *Parish Catechetical Ministry* by Robert J. Hater, published by Benziger Publishing Company, Mission Hills, California.

Excerpts from THE JERUSALEM BIBLE, copyright © 1966 by Darton, Longman & Todd, Ltd. and Doubleday & Company, Inc. Used by permission of the publisher.

International Standard Book Number: 0–87793–434–7

Library of Congress Catalog Card Number: 90-82056

Cover and text design by Katherine Robinson Coleman.

Printed and bound in the United States of America.

Dedicated
with love and gratitude
to
Olivia L. Hater,
my mother,
celebrating her 80th birthday
July 20, 1990.

Mom's love strengthens me,
her wisdom inspires me,
her intelligence encourages me,
and her faith gives me life.

Contents

Preface

News That Is Good: Evangelization for Catholics is a refreshingly new, prayerful view of evangelization, God and the people of God. This fine work is a meditation for Catholics who wish to evangelize the active Catholic community before evangelizing other communities. It is not a handbook on how to evangelize, though the final chapter lays out general principles for evangelizing the active Catholic.

The book is written for those responsible for pastoral practice and teaching, that they might find in evangelization the energy and the dynamism to proclaim God's presence in family, society, work and church. A rounded understanding of Catholic evangelization with its call to conversion must ground all ministry in the church today.

News That Is Good is positive, inspiring and challenging, as evangelization writing should be. A book like this would not have been written 20 years ago when the concept of evangelization, or faith sharing, was at its lowest ebb in the history of the church in America. Thanks to Pope Paul VI's apostolic exhortation, *Evangelization in the Modern World* (which is quoted generously throughout the book), and thanks to the work and writings of a growing band of apostolic Catholics like Father Robert Hater, the vast majority of active Catholic parishioners today are not embarrassed by Catholic evangelization. Rather, they see evangelization as a worthy work that should be given higher priority in the life of the church, even though, sad to note, only a very small handful of Catholic laity actually share their faith and invite their friends, relatives and neighbors to investigate the Catholic family of believers.

It is interesting to note that Father Hater's book will be appearing about the time the church celebrates the 15th anniversary of *Evangelization in the Modern World*, the magna charta of Catholic evangelization, the single most important work to spark the renewed interest in evangelization in America. Father

Hater's book is witness to a new consciousness arising within the American Catholic people that, by the fact of baptism, we are all called to evangelize, to build God's kingdom on earth.

No significant movement in the church exists without a body of literature to report on the movement, to reflect on the movement, to stretch the imagination and to challenge creative thinking. *News That Is Good* is a significant contribution to the growing body of literature on Catholic evangelization in America, as we Catholics expand our understanding of the beauty as well as the complexity of evangelization.

In his book, Father Hater remains faithful to the title of the book and to his intention in writing it. He touches very lightly on the other four great beneficiaries of evangelization (inactive Catholics, unchurched Americans, ecumenical evangelization and interreligious evangelization). He presents a very balanced view of the Rite of Christian Initiation of Adults (RCIA) as it affects both active Catholics and those seeking full union with the Catholic church.

Catholics who read and reflect on this book will lay a solid foundation for the evangelization of active Catholics — and the evangelization of all who need to hear the good news of salvation in Jesus Christ as proclaimed for two thousand years by the Catholic church.

Rev. Alvin A. Illig, C.S.P.
Director, Paulist National
Catholic Evangelization Association

Introduction

Spring's fresh air pours into my open window as I begin this work on evangelization. The chirping and singing of a robin outside promises new life and stimulates my recollections of family, God, Jesus, church and other faiths. It all seems fitting. After all, evangelization captures belief in God's presence, life's unity, human love, the paschal mystery of Jesus, and the Christian community's concern for hurting people.

The purpose of this book is to clarify the meaning of evangelization within the Catholic community, where the term often takes on negative connotations. This may be strongly influenced by the "evangelism" of the fundamentalist television preachers. Evangelization is the invitation to share faith, and conversion is the "amen." The televangelists' invitation to share faith stresses conversion as a once-and-for-all definitive event. For Catholics, however, conversion is an ongoing process that invites people to enter more deeply into the mystery of God's love as manifested in the death and resurrection of Jesus. It's a community or a person saying "so be it" to God's message on many occasions during life. It's a lifelong process focusing on the kingdom of God.

Put in its simplist terms Catholic evangelization announces God's loving message in word and deed again and again. It's the proclamation of God's presence in family, society, work and church through example and words. A parent's love, a neighbor's compassion, an employer's business practice, an employee's work, a parish's welcome, the teaching of Jesus' message and the witness of a good life — all are evangelization. All proclaim God's presence.

News That Is Good is intended not only to help dispel confusion in the Catholic community about the meaning of evangelization, but also to encourage Catholics to establish an evangelical spirit. It is intended primarily for pastoral ministers — priests, parish ministers, coordinators of Catholic evangelization, directors of religious education, school principals and teachers, renewal coordinators, RCIA directors — anyone responsible for directing pastoral practice and teaching. It blends stories, pastoral insights, and theological wisdom in a practical way, and can be used by other readers as well. Hopefully, its spiritual and pastoral approach will help readers see God's presence in life more clearly.

Chapter One defines Catholic evangelization and Chapter Two relates it to the kingdom of God. Chapter Three roots Catholic evangelization in the broader context of life, which is the focal point of God's ongoing revelation. Chapter Four situates Catholic evangelization in the dialogue between family, world and church. Chapter Five describes the characteristics of Catholic evangelization.

Chapter Six studies evangelization and conversion. It considers the modes of God's revealing presence, clarifies the meaning of conversion, looks at individual and communal conversion and considers methods to help facilitate conversion. Chapter Seven studies evangelization and ministry. Chapter Eight offers suggestions about what Catholics can learn from the popularity of fundamentalism. Chapter Nine reflects on evangelization and spirituality as rooted in the kingdom of God. Chapter Ten offers pastoral suggestions for evangelization in parish life.

I hope this book will help carry out Jesus' call to proclaim God's love in our time. The robin's song I hear recalls this love. May similar memories move readers to recognize God's presence in all of creation.

ONE

Defining Catholic Evangelization

Jim and Sally live in a small Midwestern town. Now retired, they enjoy walking through shops, greeting old friends and meeting new ones. One afternoon they saw a young woman walking alone. She was a newcomer. They welcomed her. The woman's name was Connie.

Soon Connie, Jim and Sally sat in an ice cream parlor. Connie was sad, so Jim and Sally invited her to their home. After a nice dinner and personal conversation, Connie expressed tremendous gratitude, then told them she must leave town. Bill and Sally never saw her again.

On Holy Thursday, five years later, they received a package. Opening it up, Sally found a small frayed teddy bear and a letter which read:

Dear Sally and Jim,

It's been a long time since we met. Remember five years ago when you bought me ice cream, invited me to your home for dinner and listened to me? I was depressed but never told you why. The evening before, I learned I was pregnant. Unmarried and 19, I panicked, ran away, got off the bus in your town and thought of killing myself. Your love, concern and prayers changed my mind. When I left, Jim said, "Trust God, and you will be okay." Those words, your kindness and God's help saved my life. Enclosed find a small teddy bear. It is frayed and worn. This was my baby Erica's first toy. I want you to have it, as a reminder that two people, myself and little Erica, owe you our lives. Thank you for giving us life. We are now fine. I pray that I can do for others what you have done for us.

Love,
Connie

Were Sally and Jim evangelizers? The answer is yes if we understand the term in light of the Second Vatican Council.

Before Vatican II, "evangelization" was not commonly used in Catholic pastoral practice or theology. However, the Council and Pope Paul VI's encyclical *Evangelization in the Modern World* established new directions for our understanding of kingdom and church.

Pope Paul stresses Jesus' life and ministry as the chief content of evangelization. Consequently, to appreciate evangelization, one must look to the Christian scriptures, which reveal Jesus' evangelizing activities. In his encyclical the pope lists these as: Jesus' incarnation, his miracles and teachings, the gathering of the disciples, the sending out of the apostles, his crucifixion and resurrection, and the permanence of his presence in the Christian community. These remind us that evangelization is much more than "words." It requires the active witness of faith, hope and charity.

For Catholics, the word *evangelization* is still not commonly understood. This came home to me last year when I taught an upper-level ministry course at a university. The class topic was evangelization. I began by asking the students their reaction to the word. Their responses, mostly negative, surprised me. The vast majority associated it with fundamentalism, especially the preaching of the televangelists. "Why talk about evangelization in a class on Catholic ministry?" asked one student. "Is that what we are about?" Most students had no idea what evangelization meant. Only one or two vaguely grasped its meaning.

Because of this unfamiliarity, it is important to clarify its meaning before nuancing and developing aspects of evangelization.

The church refers to evangelization in two ways in recent documents. It uses it in a holistic sense in the encyclicals *Evangelization in the Modern World* and *On Catechesis in Our Time*, and uses it in a more restricted sense in the *General Catechetical Directory*, the *National Catechetical Directory* and the *Rite of Christian Initiation of Adults*. This book follows the holistic use.

The Holistic Approach to Evangelization

A preparatory document for the 1973 World Synod on Evangelization describes it as "the activity whereby the church proclaims the gospel, so that the faith may be aroused, may unfold, and may grow."[1] Pope Paul VI, in *Evangelization in the Modern World*, states, "For the church, to evangelize means bringing the Good News into all strata of humanity, and through its influence, transforming humanity from within and making it new" (*Evangelization in the Modern World*, no. 18).

In this context, evangelization can be described as a *process fostering ongoing conversion within the Christian community that seeks to initiate people ever more deeply into the mystery of God's love (the kingdom), as it is manifested most fully in the dying and rising of Jesus*. This description contains several important notions.

First: Evangelization is the invitation to accept the good news of God's love. Evidence of God's love, which first comes from life itself and sets the stage for Jesus' revelation, can be called implicit evangelization. Examples include the beauty of creation, the love from a parent, the compassionate listening of

---

1. "The Evangelization of the Modern World," pp. 1–2. Working Paper for the International Synod on Evangelization, 1973. Published by the U.S. Catholic Conference, Washington, D.C.

a friend, and social concerns of a parish. Even if Jesus' name is not mentioned, evangelization happens in implicit ways, thus preparing for more explicit manifestations of Jesus' saving word. Explicit evangelization proclaims the role of Jesus, God, kingdom and church in God's plan of salvation and gives deeper insights into the God already present in implicit evangelization. This may happen formally in a church, classroom or study group, informally at home, with friends or in the workplace. Christians respond to this explicit proclamation through service, and celebrate it through worship and prayer. Implicit and explicit evangelization foster ongoing conversion.

Second: Conversion happens between God and individuals within community. Conversion is always communitarian, for people learn their deepest values from others. Even when conversion occurs in solitary moments, it happens because the person has lived in a family, communicated with friends and worked with associates who have influenced the individual.

Third: Evangelization seeks to initiate people ever more deeply into the mystery of God's love. This initiation requires explicit proclamation of the gospel. Recently, a friend told me that after an accident he tried to discover how God was speaking to him through his sickness. The crucifix was the only symbol that gave him hope and a reason to go on. As he grew to appreciate how it connected with his suffering, the scripture took on new meaning. Reading the story of Christ's passion, meditating on the crucifix, and celebrating the Eucharist evangelized him in a way that nature or a friend's love never could have.

Fourth: Evangelization shows that God's love is manifested most fully in the death and resurrection of Jesus. During my friend's sickness, he learned how Jesus' death reflected God's love. Soren Kierkegaard describes this love, climaxed on the cross, as "the supreme paradox." A God dying for creatures makes no sense to reason but becomes a source of salvation through faith. Jesus being raised from the dead by the Father is the final testimony, affirming that no matter what conclusions a person might be tempted to draw from suffering, disappointment or frustration, Christian faith says God's love transcends death and promises eventual happiness.

Evangelization, a lifelong process, is a response to God's call to proclaim the good news of the kingdom in word and deed. It is not a separate ministry but is central to all ministries. Evangelization is the heart of ongoing conversion, in which God's word doesn't change, but people's ability to hear it changes, depending on their age and circumstances. This understanding differs from the evangelism of the fundamentalists, which emphasizes hearing God's word and accepting Jesus Christ once and for all in a definitive moment of conversion and salvation.

The risen Lord evangelizes through the Christian community. For the church, evangelization means "first of all to bear witness, in a simple and direct way, to God revealed by Jesus Christ, in the Holy Spirit; to bear witness that in his Son God has loved the world — that in His Incarnate Word he has given being to all things and has called men to eternal life" (*Evangelization in the Modern World*, no. 26). Consequently, evangelization means that people hear the good news of God's forgiveness because we forgive; that people see Christian hope because they witness our hope; and that people celebrate divine friendship because we dare to be friends.

Evangelization is a process whereby the living Lord is experienced in flesh and blood — in the joys and tears of everyday life — because we are bold enough to live as if God is our loving Father. Evangelical witness "will always contain — as the foundation, center and at the same time summit of its dynamism — a clear proclamation that, in Jesus Christ, the Son of God made man, who died and rose from the dead, salvation is offered to all men, as a gift of God's grace and mercy" (*Evangelization in the Modern World*, no. 27).

Evangelization is the kingdom in action, telling society that the word of Jesus is alive. Every day, family members proclaim God's word to one another through patience, sacrifice and generosity. Workers and managers proclaim God's word in the workplace by following gospel values of justice and fairness. Churches support and assist members through preaching, teaching, liturgy, counseling and generous giving to the marginalized.

Evangelization is the lifeblood of Christian life and ministry. As an ongoing activity of the Christian community, it includes the initial proclamation of the word, as well as the various pastoral ministries that nourish this initial proclamation. Evangelization receives further specification in the ministries of word, worship and service. Consequently, evangelization happens in catechesis and preaching, prayer and liturgy, and service. The following diagram of the evangelization tree portrays the holistic view of evangelization developed in this chapter.

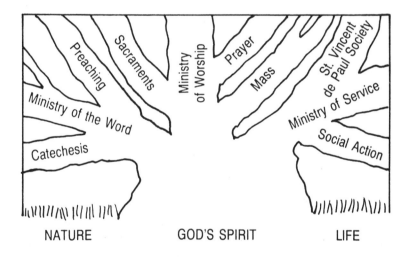

This holistic view of evangelization is also called the Convergence Model.[2] The whole tree represents the evangelization process with three chief aspects: word, worship and service. Evangelization, while rooted in nature and life, takes its nourishment from God's Spirit.

---

2. See "The Evangelizing Church," Proceedings of the NCCE Fourth Annual Conference, July 25–28, 1987. Published by the National Council for Catholic Evangelization, Cleveland, Ohio.

Restricted Approach to Evangelization

This approach sees evangelization (and sometimes pre-evangelization) as operative before a person makes a faith commitment. Its usage was popular in the 1960s and '70s, especially in catechetical and missionary work. Many Catholics, active in the church's pastoral ministries during these years, understand evangelization in this context.

The following model illustrates this approach:

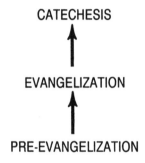

CATECHESIS

↑

EVANGELIZATION

↑

PRE-EVANGELIZATION

Pre-evangelization sets the stage for evangelization. This includes welcome, kindness, charity and social concern that prepare people to receive God's word. Once the climate is set, evangelization helps people learn about Jesus and the church. As evangelization proceeds, and people look toward a faith commitment, catechesis begins. This threefold movement is evident in the Rite of Christian Initiation of Adults. Here, evangelization and pre-evangelization set the stage. When the person chooses to become a catechumen, catechesis starts. Hence, evangelization is seen in terms of the initial proclamation of the gospel, which is directed toward conversion and is followed by catechesis. In this approach, people are evangelized before and catechized after they make an initial faith commitment.

This approach to evangelization emphasizes the importance of setting a proper climate for God's word and acknowledging a person's level of readiness. These are very important. The approach becomes problematic, however, if it dichotomizes evangelization and catechesis, which are not an either/or; namely, first evangelization, then catechesis. Rather, as the holistic approach says, catechesis is an aspect or moment in the evangelization process. The holistic and restricted approaches are acceptable forms of Catholic evangelization, but in this book we will work with and develop the holistic approach.

In proclaiming the lived reality of Jesus' dying, rising and sending of the Spirit, evangelization energizes Christian efforts, reminding people of their mission to live God's kingdom. Christian life is rooted in the lifeblood and marrow of evangelization; without it, individual or institutional efforts to proclaim God's word, celebrate it and serve others lack the dynamism promised by the good news.

TWO

Evangelization and the Kingdom

Word came to a downtown parish that Millie, a bag lady, had died and requested Catholic burial.

Shortly before the funeral liturgy began, the priest/celebrant heard noise in the church. Looking out from the sacristy he saw beggars, alcoholics, bag ladies and other street people assembling for the service.

The church filled. Unable to explain what was happening, the priest discarded his prepared homily, walked among the congregation, and said, "Welcome! Why are all of you here? Who was this woman?"

A beggar responded, "Millie was the kindest person I knew. I loved her. She was good to me." An alcoholic continued, "That's right; she taught me about Jesus and gave me her coat when I was cold." The bag ladies nodded in approval. They all loved Millie, the "Saint of the Streets." That's why they came.

Street people knew Millie, even if parish ministers did not. Sharing her possessions with the poor spoke to them of God.

Millie's story recalls the episode in the Nazareth synagogue when Jesus said, "He has sent me to bring the good news to the poor, to proclaim liberty to captives and to the blind new sight, to set the downtrodden free, to proclaim the Lord's year of favor" (Lk 4:18). Jesus' words are the heart of the kingdom, which is the heart and goal of evangelization. What then is the kingdom of God that Jesus proclaimed?

The biblical terms for kingdom — *malkuth* in Hebrew and *basileia* in Greek — are sometimes translated into English as "reign" or "rule" because "kingdom" has a male orientation. But I don't think these words capture the full impact of the biblical use.

The Hebrew and Greek words imply the power symbolized by a strong ruler or king. Such power meant the submission of servant to a master.

Jesus turned this meaning on its head by using it in a radical way. He applied a paradoxical twist to its meaning — for the follower of Christ, power means service.

> You call me Master and Lord, and rightly; so I am. If I, then, the Lord and Master, have washed your feet, you must wash each other's feet (Jn 13:13–14).

Kingdom does not imply king but man/woman in equal measure. When using "kingdom," the Christian dares to serve and to accept the total equality of man and woman, young and old, servant and master.

> You are, all of you, [children] of God through faith in Christ Jesus. All baptized in Christ, you have all clothed yourselves in Christ, and there are no more distinctions between Jew and Greek, slave and free, male and female, but all of you are one in Christ Jesus (Gal 3:26–28).

It may help to translate kingdom as "presence." The Hebrew and Christian scriptures describe this presence as freeing people from brokenness and sin and moving them toward health and wholeness. The goal of the kingdom is to give life and freedom, not death and bondage.

The kingdom of God is the key with which to understand Jesus' mission and to appreciate Catholic evangelization. A personal experience helped me see the kingdom of God in a contemporary focus.

Ben spent much of his time ministering to poor people. He resided in a two-room apartment in the inner city, surviving without salary or benefits. He had an old truck and tremendous faith in God.

He called me two weeks before Christmas, saying that the poor in Appalachia were in particularly difficult condition this year, because the government cut back certain assistance programs. He asked me to get him food, clothes and blankets to fill his truck so he could help this Christmas.

I obtained the items he requested. Sometime after Christmas we were going out for lunch and I met him at his apartment.

His austere surroundings struck me. With his simple mountain furniture it was almost as if a mountain cabin had been moved to the city. While looking around, my eyes settled on several black and white photographs hanging on the wall. The center one showed three poorly dressed women, several children, some chickens, and a dog standing in the dirt before a large, rusted tin shed. The shed was about 30 feet long, 15 feet deep, and 8 feet high. It protruded from a mountain which formed the back wall.

"Who are those women, and where is that shed?" I asked. Ben replied, "That's where we celebrated Christmas this year. Inside the shed I gave out the supplies you obtained for me. The old woman in the middle lived in a cave until three years ago. The other women and children were abandoned. They got together and started living in the shed which the coal companies used for storage."

Ben continued. "I want you to hear something." He picked up an old tape recorder and located the place he wanted on the tape. "This," he said, "is from our Christmas celebration in the tin shed." I listened. The guitarist was a bit flat and the singers off key, but from that tape came joy, peace and love like I have never experienced on any professionally produced tape. Then it struck me: "That's the way Jesus was born!"

He came among the poor in an out-of-the-way place. His first visitors were shepherds, who often had reputations as thieves. Sometimes they took food and other necessities to support themselves. Together, like the poor of the gospels, the Appalachian poor celebrated God's love and renewed their hope by listening again to the story of Jesus' birth.

Then something else hit me. For the first time I realized that the stories describing Jesus' birth and early life were written to introduce a key theme in the heart of the gospels — the kingdom of God. These stories are introductions to Jesus' kingdom message. They tell how Jesus was rejected, cast out, and broken not only in his last days, but from the beginning of his life. Jesus accepted an impoverished state to show us the depth of God's love. Because Jesus — who is God — accepted the brokenness that scriptures describe, people know that God is in the hurting, broken conditions of every person. Who, then, is the Christian God? A God who loves everyone, but is present especially with hurting, broken people, helping them become whole and holy.

Today, as in Jesus' time, many hurting, broken people struggle to survive. Their brokenness may be economic, psychological, spiritual or physical.

To better appreciate the meaning of kingdom, we should understand the following:

— Jesus was sent by God.
— His mission was to proclaim the kingdom of God.
— He did this through his ministry — that is his presence, his words and his deeds.
— The kingdom is directed toward the poor, whether they are experiencing *economic, physical, psychological* or *spiritual poverty.*
— Jesus knew poverty.
— The result of the presence of the kingdom is *healing, reconciliation* and *forgiveness.*

The poor are a special focus of God's presence. Jesus was sent to proclaim good news to the poor, salvation to sinners, and hope to those without hope. In becoming one like us, Jesus was born in poverty and experienced forms of economic, physical, psychological and spiritual poverty.

The scriptures indicate that poverty is an evil to be overcome, not a condition to be maintained. Therefore, while God is a friend of the poor, this same God desires to root poverty out. Jesus' life gives testimony to God's plan and shows he truly became one like us.

Jesus was born in a state of *economic* poverty, far from city affluence and comfort. In his adult years as a wandering preacher, he was not bound to material possessions, saying of himself, ". . . the Son of Man has nowhere to lay his head" (Mt 8:20).

Jesus also accepted *physical* poverty, which implies bodily suffering. The stories of his birth hint at the pain Jesus experienced in the difficult situation of his birth. Jesus' agony and crucifixion are supreme symbols of his willingness to embrace physical poverty.

Jesus' *psychological* anguish must have been intense. Throughout his life, people misunderstood him. They threw him out of the Temple, opposed his teaching, harassed his disciples and accused him of blasphemy. Judas betrayed him and Peter denied him. Jesus agonized in the garden and cried on the cross. Psychological or emotional poverty permeated his life.

Jesus was not exempt from *spiritual* poverty, either. Sin is one kind of spiritual poverty. Jesus never sinned, but he accepted the condition of human sinfulness in order to save the world.

Lack of meaning is also spiritual poverty. Consciousness of his mission gave meaning to Jesus' life. But when near death he questioned the meaning of what was happening to him when he cried out, "My God, my God, why have you deserted me?" (Mk 15:34). Jesus suffered rejection and isolation, leading to questions such as the one he uttered to his Father. But when despair tempted him, Jesus turned to God, saying, "Father, into your hands I commit my spirit" (Lk 23:46).

The gospels indicate clearly that Jesus assumed the human condition. God's presence, reflected in Jesus' teaching on the kingdom, was central to his life and ministry. He became poor to vanquish poverty. His example affords hope for anyone immersed in poverty, for Jesus teaches that poverty is never the end.

Healing, reconciliation and forgiveness are the results of the presence of God's kingdom. When these happen, God is there. To learn to what degree a parish, school, family or individual lives the kingdom message, one might observe their willingness to reconcile or forgive.

Jesus says to the Pharisees, "Which of these is easier: to say, 'Your sins are forgiven you' or to say, 'Get up and walk'? But to prove that the Son of Man has authority on earth to forgive sins," — he said to the paralyzed man — "I order you: get up, and pick up your stretcher and go home" (Lk 5:23–24).

Reconciliation always brings miracles, for whenever life's broken pieces are mended, peace follows. A miracle happens when people say amen to urgings of the God-always-present encouraging them to forgive. Then they begin to put the pieces back together.

Reconciliation, when used generically, means putting the pieces back together, establishing peace. Closely associated with healing, reconciliation can happen in economic, physical, psychological and spiritual poverty as individuals and groups are healed. Sometimes this implies reconciliation with oneself after making a mistake. At other times, it means reconciliation with another person. It can also refer to reconciliation with God. Usually being reconciled with self, others and God happens together.

Forgiveness, one form of reconciliation, may be necessary because of misunderstandings, mistakes or sin. Jesus associates forgiveness with sin, which blocks the relationship with God.

Jesus' resurrection is the supreme sign of reconciliation with God through the forgiveness of sin. God raised Jesus from the dead as a final testimony to his mission and ministry. The early Christians realized the significance of reconciliation and forgiveness more clearly after Jesus' resurrection. This realization enabled them to include in the Christian scriptures many testimonies to the power of reconciliation and forgiveness.

Jesus' miracles symbolize God's desire to overcome poverty and brokenness. Miracles do happen. People don't cause them, God does. But people aid in God's creative desire to make all things whole. Reconciliation implies any efforts, including miracles, that bring wholeness to an individual or group. The gospels describe Jesus' healing, reconciling ministry in stories such as the man born blind, Peter's mother-in-law and Zacchaeus. In each instance, new life enters a person when healing occurs.

Reconciliation, including forgiveness, is not easy. While on earth, humans dwell in the kingdom of the "now," where God's presence with imperfect people helps them become whole. This takes time. Often a person can only say, "God, help me become whole, I hurt so much," or "God, help me repair my broken marriage or friendship," or "God, help me be reconciled with my child."

Only in heaven will healing, reconciliation and forgiveness be complete. Here, there will be no more suffering, no more pain, no more hurt.

Church and the Kingdom of God

Creation, brought to its highest point in Jesus, continues in Christ's earthly body, the church, which exists to continue his mission and ministry. This realization dawned on the disciples at Pentecost as the Holy Spirit illuminated Jesus' followers and helped them see how the Christian community is the body of Christ, responsible to proclaim the kingdom under the guidance of the Spirit. The church does this through its ministry — its corporate and individual witness including teaching, good example, worship, prayer and social ministry.

The church exists to bring God's kingdom to completion. Like the life of Jesus, it is directed toward the poor and broken, offering them healing, reconciliation and forgiveness.

Poor

Like Jesus, the church brings the kingdom to those who are economically, physically, psychologically or spiritually poor. These conditions take distinct forms today.

Much of the world is economically impoverished as millions of people, lacking adequate food, clothing and shelter, are left to a cruel fate. Some Christians try to help by giving money and goods to the poor or by volunteering their services. This kind of giving, good and necessary in itself, aids many people. But it can subtly camouflage real poverty issues, for charity will never alleviate poverty; only justice will.

More and more Christians are accepting the kingdom's call to work for justice and oppose the economic, social and political systems that keep people impoverished. The presence of God calls for all Christians — political leaders, business executives, workers and family members — to carry out their mission to help alleviate economic poverty.

Physical poverty refers to bodily impairments caused by such things as sickness, accidents, handicaps of birth or the aging process. The gospel recounts the many stories of Jesus encountering and healing those who suffered from physical poverty. The kingdom proclaimed by his life and ministry promises God's presence through his church to those suffering from physical poverty.

Marcia is a dormitory placement coordinator at a large university. Seven students came to her office the first day of the fall semester demanding to be moved from the dormitory they were assigned to. "Why?" Marcia inquired. Bill, a strong, athletic man, spoke for the group. "The people there are different. Some don't speak right, others can't walk, still others are hunched over." Marcia realized immediately that the students had been assigned to the handicapped dormitory.

She told them she would get their rooms changed, but it would take about a month. Sue, one of the seven students, was adamant, saying, "We want out now!" Finally the group reluctantly agreed to stay in this dorm until changes could be arranged. They were to check back with Marcia in a month.

About three weeks later Marcia was eating dinner in a popular restaurant. She heard laughing and hilarity in an adjoining room. Looking through the door, she saw the students who had come to her office. Sue was helping a handicapped girl cut her food. Another one of the seven assisted a young man with his vegetables. After some time, Bill raised a glass and said, "Let's toast God for bringing us together." Then, turning to a severely handicapped student, he said, "Happy Birthday, Ed!"

Marcia waited for the students to return to her office. One month passed, then a few more, and finally the year ended. They never returned to change their dormitory. These students learned from the gospel message, "Happy are the poor in spirit" (Mt 5:3). The physically handicapped students taught the other seven about life.

Catholic evangelizers can learn valuable lessons from this story. When reaching out to help, more than the handicapped are blessed.

Psychological poverty is also widespread in modern society. Life's fast pace, the pressures to adequately balance work and family life, the widespread use of drugs, divorce and other social ills drive people to emotional upheaval and illness. Too often life becomes a series of chores to be fulfilled rather than an exciting mystery to be celebrated.

Some years ago a college student responded negatively to my efforts to help him in class. During the first four weeks he missed many classes and most assignments. When I asked him why, he said, "I'm not interested in this class. I took it because I have to. After school I work to pay for my education. This takes much of my time." Halfway through the term, I talked to him again. By this time he was doing even less work and rarely came to class. I told him I couldn't pass him unless he improved. He became adamant and said he didn't care.

Finally I threw my grade book on the desk and said, "Bill, I don't care about your grades, but I do care about you. Won't you please let me be your friend?" Upon hearing this, this large young man fell on me and sobbed like a baby. Finally he looked up and said, "Father, you are the first person in my life that ever asked me to be his friend." He never missed another class, made up his work, and got a "B."

Bill suffered psychological poverty — a gnawing loneliness — that paralyzed him in an almost meaningless life. He needed encouragement and a friend. Many people are like Bill and Jesus invites us to reach out to them. Evangelization gives this kind of witness to help further God's kingdom.

People who suffer from mental breakdowns or are mentally handicapped also experience psychological poverty. These individuals need understanding but also invite Christians to gain a deeper understanding of the gospel message.

Years ago a priest, Joe, had a mental breakdown in the missions at age 28 which debilitated him the rest of his life. This once athletic, humorous, brilliant man was never again the same. He tried several assignments over the years, but was unable to function. Eventually he returned to the monastery, where he offered daily Mass, prayed, and walked the streets of the town talking to people.

When Joe died, his family and members of his order were amazed as hundreds of people filled the church, most of them unknown, poor and ordinary. After the funeral the family discovered that Joe was a spiritual advisor for many people in the town near his monastery. He did more than just greet people in the stores or sit on their porches: They sought his advice, which they regarded as sacred.

The religious community was also surprised to learn that many sisters and brothers in the community went to him for spiritual direction. Truly, Joe was a "saint." Those living with him over the years treated him patiently and kindly, but few realized how God used Joe to bring good news to so many people. In his brokenness, God's favor was revealed. How important for Catholic evangelization that we recognize God's special presence with mentally handicapped people!

Spiritual poverty is rampant as people search desperately for meaning. The deepest spiritual poverty is sin, which interferes with the God-human relationship. By freely turning away from God through serious sin, a person is cut off from the deepest wellsprings of grace and meaning.

Sins committed years ago often continue to gnaw at people. Some believe their sins are unforgivable. Failing to appreciate Jesus' good news of forgiveness, they live in quiet desperation.

Once a female hospital chaplain told me that she sat daily with an old man belonging to no church. Near death, he lingered on. One afternoon he shared with her an offense he had committed against his children years ago. He cried. The chaplain said she believed God forgave him. He answered, "Do you really believe God forgave me?"

"Yes," the chaplain replied. Great peace came over him, as they prayed for God's forgiveness. He died a few hours after she left.

Because of the world's sinful condition and life's imperfections, people experience other kinds of spiritual poverty as well. One is spiritual meaninglessness, indicated by a hollowness in life. In a world where money, power and sex take precedence over justice, peace and love, people's deepest needs for affection, security, happiness and meaning often go unattended.

The spiritual yearning for love, understanding, relaxation and play will not go away. Life is out of hand when play or visiting a friend becomes a chore in an appointment book, carried out on a schedule. The ultimate cannot be programmed. No wonder the Hebrew scriptures say, "Remember the sabbath day and keep it holy" (Ex 20:8). The first creation account tells us, "God blessed the seventh day and made it holy, because on that day he rested after all his work of creating" (Gn 2:3). This reminds people to take time for God, themselves and others. Genesis gives people a clue on how to put life in better balance. Keep Sunday holy — praise God, pray, enjoy family and friends, relax and have fun.

I learned about life's priorities from Sam, a student I had in a college course.

After the first day of class, Sam, a handsome, strong-looking student, approached me. "Father, I'll have to miss one class every other week. Is that okay?"

I replied, "Not really, unless you have a good reason." Sam explained that he had a rare blood disease and came close to death two years before.

"Every other week they bring me to the hospital and replace my blood, so I can live for two more weeks." I was stunned as I looked at this man with the physique of a football player. I said, "Sam, you'd better miss class every other week."

As the class progressed, Sam's maturity impressed the students. He never mentioned his ailment. A month before the end of the semester he wrote a reflection paper. After reading it, I asked him to share it with the class. The day he did, Sam began by rolling up his long-sleeved shirt that always covered his arms. Then he bent his arms and said, "Look at my arms! They are like leather." As he pounded them, they resembled the sleeves of a leather jacket. "They are like this," he continued, "because hospital personnel have stuck hundreds of needles into them to give me blood. Now my arms will take no more needles, and they must find other places in my body to put the needles." Shocked by the appearance of Sam's arms and by his initial comments, the students listened in rapt attention to his story. At one point he picked up the reflection paper he wrote for me and read:

What does life mean to you? Is life something you put on every morning like your clothes and walk out the door not giving it another thought? Or is life something you put on like your clothes and walk out the door making the most of every second, of every hour, of every day?

The date is September 12, 1980. The location is a city hospital in St. Louis, Missouri.

As I walk down the hospital corridor, I see a young girl smile at me. We start talking and I tell her about my illness and she says she has a tumor at the edge of her brain. Tomorrow she would have surgery. Sally is only 12 and knows she will either be okay or have a malignancy or come out of surgery paralyzed. It seems so unreal, for she is so young. I almost wish Jesus was there and I could beat on his chest and ask, "Why?"

Sally didn't expect to see me the next morning. They wheel her around the corner where I stand and stop the cart. Sally puts out her arms, we hug, and she looks at me as if to say, "I'm ready." Then they wheel her into the elevator.

When I turn from the elevator, I see the radiator. I kick it so hard that if it wasn't attached to the wall, I would have kicked it right out the window. When I kick the radiator, I look up at the ceiling and shout, "Why? She's only 12! And why did I nearly die several years ago? One day I played in an all-star football game; two days later I woke up sick, and ten days later I discovered I had a rare blood ailment."

Sally is fine today, and I continue to amaze the doctors. Through my experiences I have learned something about the "why" of suffering. Even more, I have learned to appreciate life. My message is simple; "Make the most of life! Live it to the fullest." For there are people of all ages who would give anything just to walk up the street, just to live a near-normal life.

I know the meaning of suffering, for I have almost died four times. Through suffering I yearn for life. Nothing means more to me than to wake up to see the light and the smog, for I have learned to appreciate just being alive.

Sam had a tremendous influence on the students. He lived a hopeful message. I never saw him after the semester ended, but his words remain with me, especially his final remarks on the last class day: "Miracles do happen! They aren't caused by you or me, but by God. So trust God, no matter what might happen."

Faith, like Sam's, roots spiritual meaning, which is the foundation of human activities.

The message of Sam's story is that no effective evangelization happens unless it is rooted in the spiritual. If dioceses, parishes and individuals live the spiritual message of the gospels, Christians will be inspired to counter today's secular message with a God-centered message that offers ultimate meaning in a functional world. The kingdom of God happens when people turn away from the alienation caused by functional gods to discover healing, health and wholeness in God's love and human compassion.

Healing, Reconciliation and Forgiveness

Frequently people working for the church become disillusioned by politics, infighting and turf building. While they operate under the banner of Christ, the results of the presence of God — healing, reconciliation and forgiveness — may not be evident.

Once I moderated a parish council meeting in a parish that was split into two rival factions. We met on Sunday in a retreat setting. After 15 minutes, intense group hostility made it impossible to discuss any significant issues. I interrupted the meeting and said, "Stop! Look at what's happening. Since I am coordinating this meeting, I recommend two options. First, go home and enjoy the beautiful afternoon; there is no need to continue this way. Second, go aside for two hours, ask God to enlighten us, pray for forgiveness and then reassemble. I don't know if we should celebrate Eucharist. If we can't forgive, what meaning will the Mass have, for is it not a remembrance of the kingdom in our midst?"

I asked which option they preferred. They refused to admit defeat and did not want to go home. So we went off for several hours. At 5:00 p.m. the group gathered in the chapel and discussed attitudes and actions. They wanted to celebrate Mass, eat dinner and meet that evening. I felt God's presence within the group moving them to reconciliation. We assembled from 7:30 to 9:00 p.m. Their outlook changed. I hope this continued after they returned home.

At times, people find it difficult to see Jesus' example of reconciliation and forgiveness in our communities. Parishioners often become disillusioned at the lack of charity in church leaders who are supposed to symbolize Jesus' message. The kingdom of God is gauged by the presence of forgiveness. God invites humans to re-create the world and society. For Christians, this means the constant call to reconciliation.

Evangelization demands a reconciling community. Christians cannot expect neighbors or work associates to become church members when love and forgiveness are not evident in parishes, organizations or schools. Today, many people enter the church through the Rite of Christian Initiation of Adults. While involved in this process, catechumens usually experience charity in the small Christian community that develops. But what happens after reception into the church? Many become disillusioned when they fail to experience a similar response in the parish community.

Evangelization focuses on the kingdom, which goes beyond church membership or boundaries. An evangelist is a reconciling person, reaching out to the poor, whatever their religion, nationality or economic condition, and inviting them to experience God's love. Catholic evangelization is creation-centered, reaching out to people and helping them to be reconciled to themselves, others and God. If evangelization becomes too ecclesial or church-centered, it misses Jesus' focus on the kingdom and his desire to reconcile all creation to God and runs the risk of developing into narrow, one-sided proselytization. Catholic evangelists invite others to become church members, not to swell parish ranks, but because they believe the church community is the best way for people to become Christlike and thus more fully human.

THREE

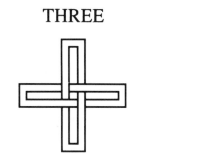

Evangelization, Creation and Life

For early civilizations, trying to understand life without linking it to creation was impossible. They returned to their creation stories to address life's meaning. Basic beliefs were revealed as the community learned the relationship between gods, spirits, people and nature. These stories acknowledged human limitations, suffering and death, and pointed to human dependency on powers greater than earthly ones.

In the 20th century, though, most people have become increasingly divorced from nature and an understanding of creation. A child living in a New York concrete jungle may be awestruck by the large trees in Central Park. A suburban child who knows nothing but artificial light may never experience the mystery and terror of dark. And yet, the same energies that pulsated through early cave dwellers move people today.

To appreciate the way Catholic evangelization, rooted in the kingdom preached by Jesus, reveals God's good news, we need to understand that creation and life itself are at the heart of God's communication with us. This chapter stresses that God's creative activity continues in partnership with nature and with

35

human endeavors. Several personal testimonies may help to illustrate this.

For the Lakota Indians, a "vision quest" involves a ritual in which a dream or vision gives direction to an individual's life. The Lakotas believe that an individual discovers the heart of God's self revelation in one's own story.

Before speaking to the tribe, a Lakota leader often shares a personal vision quest. This sharing creates a climate of trust, freedom and understanding. Sharing spiritual experiences reveals the path that has brought a person to God and has influenced one's life direction.

Perhaps every person has a special moment of revelation. Mine happened when I was 15.

> Every day I walked home from high school, usually with three or four friends. This day I was alone. I came down to the bottom of St. Lawrence Avenue and began to walk up the other side of the hill. The sun glistened in the bright spring afternoon. Crisp air, new tree buds and a pesky squirrel surrounded me. Having walked about 50 feet up the hill, I stood under an elm tree with a thick bush on the right. Suddenly a powerful presence surrounded me. I stopped and looked into the tree. The sparkling sunshine through the new green life seemed to say, "Bob, I have something special for you to do with your life." I felt warm, at peace and unafraid. I felt whole, together, loved. For a moment, my adolescent insecurities, scruples and fears ceased. The place where I stood was holy ground. The episode lasted no more than ten seconds, but 40 years later I remember it as if it happened yesterday.

While this did not elicit thoughts of a priestly vocation at that moment, I realized in this brief encounter with the divine that life has meaning and purpose. I also saw how we are guided by forces far greater than the chemical or physical laws I studied in school. My adolescent vision quest helped me appreciate that God speaks to individuals through nature.

During my childhood Dad and Mom encouraged me to love nature. In the woods behind our home we played, dug small caves, observed animals and experienced changing seasons. Dad taught me to plant seeds and cultivate tender flowers. Helping him work in the garden, repair broken trees and cut grass linked me with life's ultimate dimension.

Seminary education halted this process. It almost seemed that I left nature and family behind in the crush of academic studies, rigorous discipline, structured prayer life and isolation from the world. My early years as a priest continued this pattern. Then something happened that brought me back to reality.

I taught in the seminary for one year during the late 1960s. A week before my second year was to begin, I was in an automobile accident. Four days later I lost most of my strength. This strong, athletic, smart and confident man did not recover. Depression set in. No one knew what was wrong. I cancelled classes and often sat alone in my room for 16 hours a day, wondering if I would ever recover. Embarrassed, I avoided people, too sick to enjoy their company. Slowly but surely, I was stripped and emptied.

Then, in 1979, while I was on sabbatical, my father became critically ill. I returned to be with him and Mom the remainder of the year. During Dad's final illness I wrote a piece describing how trees and fragile plant life revealed God's presence to me during these two diffcult periods in my life.

> During the years of my intense sickness, I walked through the woods and admired the strength and struggle of trees. Tulip poplars soared in straight lines above cedars and pines. Oaks stood firm in tornadoes and squalls. Black locusts, brittle and uneven when alive, became like concrete when dried out. I went to the woods whenever I felt tired, nervous or hurt, often walking for hours, broken and depressed, not knowing where to go or what to do.

> I felt the pain of the trees in their struggle to survive. Hardwood trees eventually conquer softwoods in their quest for light. But hardwood trees need cedars and brush to prepare their seedlings. Cedars and brush need grass to cool off the earth. All are in harmony. None give up the struggle until the proper time.

When Dad's sickness came, I stopped going to the trees for a while. When I returned to them, I had changed, even if the trees remained. My old friend, the apple tree, was still there, as were the oaks and walnuts. But I didn't look at them. Instead I looked to their feet and saw the earth, flowers and tiny insects that keep the trees alive. I realized that without the smallest, the largest do not live. My perceptions changed from strength to weakness, delicacy and fragility.

I looked back at the path I created when walking in the grass and observed the cracked plants, broken daisies and tiny wild roses. I peeked under fallen trees and saw miniature gardens of moss and wild flowers. I stood transfixed every time I discovered a wild flower, which became my new symbol of life in the woods. It didn't matter if I knew the names of my small friends. What, after all, is a moss or flower's name? It is only an artificial label signifying a deeper reality. And the deeper reality is what really counts — a reality expressing beauty, mystery, peace, order and hope. The deeper reality tells us about an unspoken presence in a gentle breeze, a ray of light and a touch of beauty — a presence forever constant, yet always elusive.

As I walked through the woods, now looking down at small fragile life rather than up toward my ancient friends, the trees, I almost said, "Pardon me, my big friends, for neglecting you for a while. My experience with my father causes me to look at those moments of life where waiting, not competition, fragility, not strength, smallness, not bigness, rule. Thank you for sustaining me in the past. Now I look below you at the simple life-giving realities that made you, me and Dad possible."

Flowers became my life symbols. I meditated upon them for hours, seeing there the deepest life reality. I felt God's immense love sustaining the wild daisy or rose. The delicacy of a thousand flowers, names unknown to me, pointed to countless people, nameless faces. Often I passed by without recalling their delicacy or beauty. As I perceived the need to admit my limits and allow my beauty and inner self to blossom, I saw my life in a new way.

I felt like a flower must feel, almost totally dependent on external circumstances. Life became a matter of survival. Who really knows the deepest rhythms that keep us going? As I reflected on Dad and Mom, on trees and flowers, I knew it was none of us. From them, however, I discovered God at the heart of life who teaches us how few are our days. From God and from God's loved ones we gain wisdom of heart.

As I remember this experience of God's revelation through nature, I find it easier to understand how many children, adolescents, university students and adults discover God in a sunset, through a walk in the woods, through pet animals, birds and butterflies, through family life and friendship.

Many people who have profound experiences of God in nature or other people may find it difficult to participate in organized religious activities. Their communion with God challenges the institutional church to ask how well ecclesial ministry identifies itself with people's real needs and with the living God of peace, love and mercy.

How do these personal testimonies relate to evangelization? Looking back on my early life, sickness, Dad's death and other events, I realize that life itself roots the evangelization process. Grounding evangelization in ecclesial policies, programs or church community without acknowledging that its basic dynamism comes from nature, family, work and society dooms it to a shallow and futile existence. Catholic evangelization, then, needs to be integrated with the revelation of God's creative activity in every aspect of life.

Revelation Circles

The term *revelation* refers to generally accepted sources of revelation in the Catholic community (scripture and tradition), sometimes called "special" revelation, and revelation coming to individuals through nature and human communication, sometimes called "general" revelation. In this book we will use *revelation* in a broad sense, referring to any way that God communicates holiness or meaning in the world. A child's smile, a parent's touch, a sunset, a pet dog's companionship, a symphony's harmony, a computer's complexity, a friend's support, a Hindu guru's wisdom, the Koran, the Genesis creation account, the Sermon on the Mount, a theologian's research or a bishop's pastoral letter reveal the transcendent mystery in different yet complementary ways.

While we can arrive at deep insights into the God-world relationship through revelation, we need to remember that barriers to communication of this revelation exist because of God's transcendent otherness and because of human limitations. God's communication is filtered through imperfect, foggy prisms which never allow God's message to be fully understood or appreciated. No clear, exact answers exist to problems such as evil, suffering and death, or the mysteries of the world's origins, human destiny and eternal life. The best we have is a hint or suggestion.

For example, we can learn beauty from a flower, but beauty transcends flowers. We also experience it in other people, in mountains, in sunsets. Ultimately beauty hints at beauty's source, a God making possible all earthly beauty. In a similar way we learn goodness from parents, friends and colleagues. Long hours waiting, supporting and encouraging a sick child or adult reveal the goodness that lies deep within and connects an individual with God as life's source.

During an intense bout with sickness that ranged over almost ten years, I often wondered why a good God permitted suffering, depression and near despair. When personal darkness set in, I learned from the blackness and despair of Jesus' cross that God's energy calls people to life, not death. The cross became my symbol of hope. If he suffered and died, so must I; if he arose, so would I. I learned the paradox of a creature, groping toward wholeness, buoyed up by God's supportive energy.

These insights are all examples of the way revelation works in most people. They are hints, suggestions, intimations of God's presence and action in the world. They're not black-and-white absolute certainties, but they lead one closer to God.

The following model may clarify the way revelation occurs. This model presupposes that God is at the heart of creation, sustaining it and communicating with it in an ongoing way.

Although beyond creation, God is with it, constantly urging created life to move from incompleteness and brokenness to wholeness and freedom.

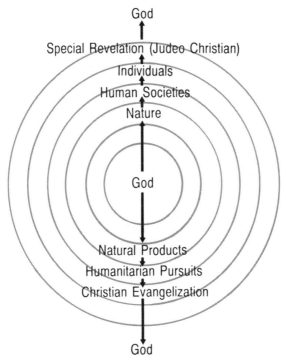

God, at the center of the circles, permeates all levels and exists beyond them. As the circles become larger, they are rooted in the smaller circles from which they take their energies. Let us first examine the upper half of the model: nature, human societies, individuals and special revelation.

Nature, including stars, planets, plants, birds and humans, mirrors God's presence and grounds all revelation. The arrow flowing from God through nature indicates the co-creative activity between Creator as ultimate life source and created nature as the means to communicate God's ongoing creative energies.

Genesis tells us that "God created man in the image of himself" (1:27). The human ability to communicate symbolically, use rational thought processes, develop science and technology, and appreciate holiness, beauty, truth, goodness and love set people apart from the rest of creation. They enable the development of *human societies*. Humans have some independence from the created universe, but when human societies distance themselves too far from the nature from which they evolved and upon which they depend, their link in communication with God becomes inadequate and distorted.

Human societies form the basis for *individual* human lives. Basic human values, such as love, patience and trust, as well as personal conscience, temperament, confidence and coping abilities are influenced by the families, friends and ethnic cultures a person experiences. Other people are often one's first revelation of God. A parent's love and sacred scripture reveal God in different ways, but both participate in God's ongoing creative activity. The diagram indicates the role humans play in God's communication with the world by the arrows that flow from God, through nature and human societies, to focus on individuals.

The outer circle indicates how God has, in various times and places, given *special revelation* to societies and individuals. Many world religions claim such revelation, often coming through a holy person (Moses, Buddha, Jesus, Mohammed). These revelations, intended to shape the community, must be accepted and authenticated by the society in question. They help illuminate the presence of God in human experience. Christianity, for example, teaches that Jesus' revelations go beyond what people could comprehend by natural means alone.

Catholic evangelization needs to ground its activity in God's presence in nature, human societies, individuals and the Judeo-Christian revelation. It must remain open to deeper insights into the Christian message that may come through dialogue with other world religions, especially their scriptures and traditions. No religion has exclusive rights to God's revelation. To claim this manifests the crassest type of haughtiness.

The lower half of the model represents the activities resulting from dialogue or interaction between the circles. The first is *natural products*. They result from people using elements of nature to produce something. Examples can range from a clay pot to a computer. The second is *humanitarian pursuits*, individuals working to better society. Examples include volunteer work in a child care center, helping a sick person and assisting tornado victims. The third is *Christian evangelization.* This results from proclaiming God's good news as revealed in the Christian scriptures in light of society's needs or individual concerns, for example, teaching children about God, celebrating Jesus' good news in liturgy and inviting Christians or non-Christians to listen to Jesus' kingdom message within the Catholic tradition.

All three categories are important for evangelization. Since God is present in nature and human societies, God is revealed here independently of scriptures or church teaching. Christians need to look for signs of God's revelation in their everyday world. A computer, television set or microscope can open up new avenues of God's revelation. They become eyes to the world, assisting the senses, reason, imagination, emotions and will to know God and life's meaning more deeply. Humanitarian activities, performed by people made in God's image, likewise manifest God, whether or not they are performed by people who explicitly believe in God.

When I was a child and teenager, working in my father's store, poor neighborhood people taught me concern for the elderly and those less fortunate than themselves. Many of these people never went to church, but I sensed God's presence in the way they looked out for an old woman living on the third floor of a tenement house and for a handicapped man who found it difficult getting to the store.

These kind actions, revealing God implicitly, are similar to Jesus' activities in reaching out to the sick and infirm. Christian evangelization, which seeks to relate Jesus' message to people's lives, is usually most effective when it integrates its approach with the way God is already implicitly present.

Discovering Meaning Through Revelation

God's revelation always comes to a person through nature, human society, special revelation or products of human ingenuity. This never happens in isolation, for each manifests God in different, yet complementary ways. The following diagram illustrates this reality:

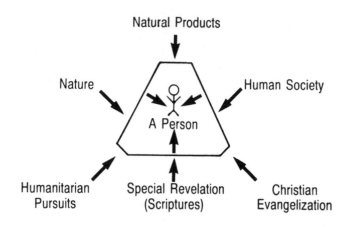

The person at the center of the triangle is molded by God's creative urges through the longest sides, namely, nature, human society and special revelation. The blunted edges of the triangle (natural products, humanitarian pursuits and Christian evangelization) result from the intersection of nature, human society and special revelation.

Every person, born through the creative energies of God present in the procreative activities of a man and a woman, is a partner with the sacred. An individual filters everything through his or her own story. This story includes a person's genes, culture, consciousness, history and activities. People are supported and energized by forces that are rooted in God and filtered through nature, human society, scripture and human products. Constantly formed through this integration, humans reach out to discover meaning in the world that shapes them. This lifelong process begins with parents and continues through family, friends and society. Every person is radically influenced by the divine energy or lack of it that comes through experience.

From the beginning of human history, people reached out to discover more than their own lives could provide in their search for God and meaning. Within this context, a society's myths, traditions and scriptures played a central role. Early cave wall paintings, scraps of parchment, ancient religious writings, statues and other artifacts indicate that people from the beginning looked beyond immediate experience of this world for ultimate answers to life's meaning, purpose and destiny. Oral traditions, still evident in Africa, South Seas Islands, and among certain American Indian tribes, confirm these written records. Both oral and written accounts describe how God(s) communicated with ancestors at creation's beginning, giving people direction and wisdom. The myths of origin disclose a tribe's approach to life by revealing basic earth secrets.

Scriptures or holy writings often form the sacred center of a community's beliefs and influence people's actions. The Hebrew-Christian scriptures, accepted as God's special revelation, have a special role in revealing the good news of God's love and salvation. The two Genesis accounts of creation set the stage for the Judeo-Christian image of God and salvation.

The seven-day creation account (Gn 1:1 — 2:4) emphasizes:

— There is one God.
— God created everything.
— Humans are created in God's image.
— The world is good.
— The sabbath is holy.

The sabbath, God's day, is holy, because Yahweh-God is holy. Holiness is God's nature and deepest being. This holiness calls people to holiness. Made in God's image, human beings are the only earthly creatures who share God's holiness, can appreciate it and can bring it into the world. This offers Christians and Jews the primary task of building a world made in the image of the all-holy God. The first Genesis story describes humans as stewards of the earth, called to act responsibly in mirroring God's creative activity. The sabbath rest, a day set aside each week for bonding with God and for personal renewal, symbolizes life's transcendent quality and invites people to look more deeply into

their lives. Evangelization, based on this biblical insight, regards
human beings as doors to holiness and ministers of peace.

The Adam and Eve account (Gn 2:5ff) emphasizes:

— Happiness means living in harmony with God (paradise
   story).
— Sin disrupts the harmony.
— Suffering and death result from sin and the human
   condition.
— God promises salvation and redemption.

The Adam and Eve story is every person's story. From
the beginning, people sinned. With sin came brokenness, pain
and death. People cannot survive alone; they need God, who
promises forgiveness and eventual happiness. This account hints
at redemption and a future messiah. Evangelization sees in this
account the importance of acknowledging friendship with God as
the means to overcome the alienation caused by sin and suffering.
Evangelization, while admitting sin's reality, urges people to turn
to God and be reconciled.

The themes of these creation accounts reappear in the historical books, the writings of the prophets, the psalms and other
writing in the Hebrew scriptures. They also ground Jesus' message, the ultimate source of good news for Christians. The
Judeo-Christian story acknowledges:

— a good world,
— a universe wounded by sin,
— the human call to help heal a broken world by sharing
   God's holiness,
— a creative plan, now continuing through human cooperation with God, moving to eventual completion.

This notion of continuing creation, humans as partners with
God in co-creation, found new meaning and impetus in the work
of Teilhard de Chardin.

Teilhard de Chardin, a Jesuit priest and scientist, lived during the first half of the 20th century. His deep spirituality, belief in God's universal presence and scientific knowledge blended to offer a new synthesis of the God-world relationship. While aspects of his work are controversial, his overall vision of God's creative activity added new insights to the relationship between God and the world.

The holistic view of creation, influenced by Teilhard's vision, includes the following elements:

— Creation is a dynamic, ongoing process.

— The universe, an unfolding reality energized by God, shares in God's ongoing creative activity.

— Humans are the special agents of co-creation. The future of the evolutionary process is in their hands. Sin can disrupt or destroy this process.

— Creation moves toward redemption in Jesus and toward a final fulfillment in what Teilhard calls the Omega Point.

— The church focuses the universe's love energy, revealed fully by Jesus, into a symphony of service and celebration.

Teilhard's vision implies that God created the world according to whatever science eventually shows to be the way the world was formed. God is within, yet beyond, the evolutionary process, which is itself always moved by God's energizing love.

Consequences for Catholic Evangelization

The universe is a continuum; one part influences another through a continuous flow of creative energy. Teilhard's views relate to insights gleaned from scripture and point to consequences for Catholic evangelization.

1. *Evangelization must take into account people's deep life energies.* These primordial needs for nurturing, affirmation, developing self-worth and understanding one's emotions influ-

ence human thought and action. Often the movement of these life energies becomes broken or blocked. Evangelization needs to tie into these wounds in people's lives, supporting and reinforcing positive life energies with Jesus' message and the church's ministry. A story from my childhood illustrates this point.

I sat with Dad and Mom on our front porch during a rain and windstorm. A small tree by the street was split down the center and nearly broken apart. After the storm, Dad and I examined it. I said, "Dad, let's help it get better." He smiled, and we got some tape, rags, string and nails. He held the tree, and I nailed it together. Then we put tar in the broken places and bound it with rags and string. Some neighborhood kids walked past, laughed, and said, "Cut it down; it will die." I watched the tree every day. In a month or so, it perked up and became strong again. It lived the remaining twenty years we were in the house.

Dad and I helped maintain the basic life energies flowing in the tree. As Catholic evangelizers, we're called to do the same for the people we meet.

2. *Catholic evangelization roots its message in God's holiness, as manifested in human lives.* Holiness influences people more deeply than knowledge. When we encounter individuals who truly live the holiness of the gospel, we are attracted to them. Only then is the stage set to hear and accept the Catholic evangelizer's message.

3. *Catholic evangelization emphasizes the ultimate more than the functional.* The Genesis creation accounts describe human beings as stewards of creation, rooted in living God's holy and loving life. We are called to respond to nature with care and respect, not with domination and abuse. People have a responsibility to build the earth, but too often this has led to functional construction based on an attitude that says science and technology can provide final answers to basic human dilemmas such as war, poverty and sickness. While science and technology play a part in building the earth, Genesis' primary message stresses

the ultimate level of love, compassion and service as the most fundamental relationship between human beings and the rest of creation.

In organized religion, an emphasis on the ultimate rather than the functional means that prayer, spirituality, compassion and love are more important than the latest computer, evangelization program, organizational structure or meeting. While a functional aspect is necessary in any structure, it never touches the deepest energies rooting a person to community or God. Unfortunately, post-Vatican II parishes, schools, dioceses and ministers have often uncritically accepted a predominantly functional appproach.

For all the efficiency and good order that follows, the ultimate sometimes gets lost in the shuffle. People's joys and struggles, where ultimate meaning is usually located, are not always orderly or efficient; often they are messy and tentative. The poor, sick and outcast usually break the models canonized by secular society and some church organizations. Catholic evangelization needs to opt for the holiness and goodness of the way of compassion over a coldly efficient organization.

4. *Catholic evangelization acknowledges creation as the ground of God's revelation.*   Evangelizers must assume a humble posture, aware that God's communication comes from many sources.   God is revealed through families, friends and society, as well as through other Christian denominations and world religions. This awareness further demands a dialogue that acknowledges these others as partners in clarifying God's message and giving meaning to the life of a community or an individual.

Catholic evangelization sees all of life as divine disclosure. Yahweh's manifestation in the history of the Jewish people, and the life of Jesus, point to a unique "God with us" relationship. Catholic evangelization recognizes this immanent yet transcendent God in the fiber of life.

Human experience continues to disclose God. Just as Moses experienced God on the mountain, we discover God when we walk through the woods or when we climb a steep hill and from its top watch a river flow to the sea. We experience God when we support a family member or pray with a friend. When we stop in church to pray and attend Mass, we experience God anew — the ever-present, alive and mysterious God who constantly invites us to new levels of meaning and comprehension. God's revelation to Moses was different from ours, but the same God and the same dynamic bring new insights and appreciation.

FOUR

Partners in Evangelization: Family, World and Church

When I was a small boy, Grandma put stale bread in the backyard for the birds, even during snowstorms. Her concern filled me with a reverence for nature. When I grew a little older, Dad and Mom read me Bible stories and taught me about Jesus. This reinforced Grandma's example from a redemption perspective. These experiences gave me a deep understanding of the kingdom of God, long before I discovered its meaning through studying the Bible.

In the same way, Catholic evangelization begins in creation, focuses on Jesus and finds expression in the community. This chapter proposes a triangle model that links family, world and church as partners in evangelization. Evangelization happens in everyday life. It is radically incarnational, which simply means that God communicates through creation. Family, world and church provide the most significant expressions of God's presence in our lives. We will consider how these three areas are part of any complete evangelization effort.

Family

Because God is first disclosed in family life, this is where evangelization begins. Family here is a broad term. We use it to include two or more people united by common bonds who share commitment, values and tradition, and whose relationship implies some degree of permanence. Besides the traditional nuclear family, this phrase includes extended, single-parent and blended families, and other intentional communities.

My own experience of family has taught me how birth, growth, joy, suffering, success, failure, life and death root one's relationship with God.

Ecclesiastes says, "There is a season for everything . . . a time for tears, a time for laughter; a time for mourning, a time for dancing" (3:1–4).

My father lay for months in a hospital bed. One cold January afternoon, Mom, my sister Mary Ann and I visited him. He smiled and asked for a wheelchair. Mom pushed him to the window.

Mary Ann and I witnessed an epiphany of love as Dad and Mom held hands and the sun illuminated them. The wrinkles and strain were transformed by the intense peace they conveyed. They spoke softly.

Mary Ann said, "Bob, seeing them together like this is worth all the long months of pain we have undergone." This moment disclosed how deep joy often comes after struggle and sacrifice.

As Dad and Mom sat there, it made no difference that his hair was not combed or she wore an older dress. They were deeply present to one another; nothing else mattered. I saw how the most beautiful experiences happen in the simplest ways, and how God discloses divine beauty when simple people radiate unaffected love. When this happens, God gives freedom, couched in liberation from sin, pleasure and worldly interests. This freedom invites healing and enables us to discover beautiful moments.

Our common story enabled us to discover these moments. Indeed, there is a season for everything. Today was our time for beautiful moments.

Not everyone experiences this kind of revelation of God within a nuclear family. But nearly everyone experiences God in a relationship of love and within a nurturing community. Another story illustrates this.

Years ago Ed, a mentally handicapped man, began attending Mass. After several months I learned from a parishioner that he wanted to receive communion. I met with Ed. He never had any formal religious training in the church, but to my surprise he knew all the basics of the Catholic faith. In further conversations, I learned the depth of his biblical understanding and sensitivity to moral issues. He desired greatly to receive communion with the community of which he was a part. Asking where he learned his deep moral values, knowledge of religious matters and positive outlook on life, Ed simply said, "From my grandmother. I lived with her for 33 years. She taught me what I know." Ed was a mystic; it would have been wrong to keep him from communion any longer. The next Sunday he joyfully received his Lord, a practice which he continues to this day.

Christian families communicate specific aspects of God's revelation by sharing the Christian faith within family life. The family is not an object "out there" to be evangelized by the church. This attitude implies that the church needs to teach families how to be families. It disregards the way God is essentially present already in a family relationship. It is far more accurate to say that families can teach church how to be church. Family and church are partners in evangelization.

Recent church documents describe the family as the "domestic church" or church of the home. The family teaches moral values, guides children, maintains religious traditions, celebrates, prays and supports its members in ways the parish cannot. The church supports, celebrates and illuminates family life through scripture, church teaching, liturgy and prayer. Parish schools and church activities help families grow in faith and link individual families with one another. Parishes best serve families by listening to their needs and responding to their requests. Often preplanned or packaged programs appeal to parish staffs but mean little to families.

Parish organizations at times pressure families to become overly involved in activities that regularly separate spouses from one another and parents from their children. Recently a woman asked my advice about joining the RCIA team. I asked about her concern. "Well, Father," she began, "I said no to the pastoral minister, but then the pastor asked me. I already work at bingo and teach volunteer religion classes for pre-school children. I don't think I can spare another evening a week. My family will suffer." I advised her to re-examine her parish commitments. Several months later she told me, "I'm pregnant and decided to drop out of all parish ministry for two years. I was over-committed, and my entire family suffered. It's hard, though, because I keep getting pressure to join this or that. I now spend more of my time with my husband and children. We are doing better as a family."

Family members, by supporting one another, bring balance into a sometimes unbalanced society. The following story of a parent's support illustrates this point.

Recently Shari, a sixth-grade girl, came home after a basketball game and laughed while telling her mom they got beat 25–4. Her mom asked, "What happened?"

"Well," Shari said, "You know Mr. Zine, our coach, is always yelling at us to work harder and harder. He told us before the game that he was videotaping all of us and we better do good because he was going to really yell at us when we saw the tapes of our mistakes. I thought, he's not going to get away with that. So I went to the girls and said, 'It's just a game; let's really mess around and act like clowns.' So we did and lost 25–4. We wanted to have fun and we did. He had a fit and was so embarrassed he threw away the tape. He never knew what happened!"

The kids, sick of an adult demanding that they play like professionals, played like kids. I sense God in the midst of this humor, clowning around in the children's hearts, howling with them at the crabby, angry coach.

Shari's mom told her they did fine — kids' sports are supposed to be fun. She also called the coach to support the children and told him to look again at his coaching methods. Imagine, though, what might have happened if Shari's mom had not supported her. Families symbolize God's support by the way they affirm their members. If evangelization doesn't happen in families, it doesn't happen anywhere.

World

World refers to the many interchanges people experience beyond their immediate family, including work (sometimes called "the marketplace"), relationships between friends, a person's social or civic involvements, neighborhood activities, school associations and the cultural and recreational activities that bring people together.

These varied relationships and activities disclose God's presence in many ways: an office secretary speaks to another employee about trusting God in a difficult situation; a neighbor reaches out in love and compassion; a person speaks morally and honestly at a civic or business meeting. The college student who says no to another's sexual advances and the business executive who refuses to compromise on a corporate deal that requires unjust treatment of minorities or aliens are both evangelizers.

A pastoral ministry class discussed ministry in the marketplace, pointing out the Christian's responsibility to act charitably, honestly and justly. One man, an engineer, said that after a retreat he realized his obligation to avoid procedures that would structurally weaken the products he designed. He followed up on this decision as his ministry. The vice-president of the corporation agreed and changed corporate policy.

Jeff, another class member, laughed when he finished. "Let me tell my story."

I was reassigned as assistant director of a large insurance office. After being there for three months, I noticed certain questionable or downright unethical practices that hurt the clients. I, too, began to speak out against these practices. My boss, first reluctant to change, finally agreed. Things went along well. The office spirit improved, and the clients were grateful. At the end of the fiscal year, we sent our new policies and reports to the main office. But our mode of operation threatened headquarters. One day three executive officers showed up unannounced, called in all the managers, and fired the entire crew. They put in new people, and today the new staff is back to the same unjust policies and procedures.

Jeff went on to explain that a Christian bold enough to evangelize in the marketplace by living and acting ethically will face tough decisions and may be rejected. Jeff said parish or Christian community support is very important for people in these situations. "Rarely," he continued, "do I hear a homily or church presentation that supports Christians hoping to sort out issues like this. We get little guidance from the church."

A dichotomy between the sacred (religion) and the secular (work and societal activities) forces people to live in two worlds. When religion, confined to church services and prayer, is disconnected from the rest of the week, many people fail to integrate the sacred and the secular. Some, like Jeff, seek this kind of integration and would welcome support from the church. Others prefer to maintain the dichotomy. For them, God has little or nothing to do with what happens in the marketplace or civic arena.

A religious group arranged a monthly program for business people, entitled "Ministry in the Marketplace," held at noon in a corporate boardroom. The sessions centered around the theme of "Growing in Relationship With Self, Others and God." It was very successful; about 60 people attended regularly. At its conclusion the participants were asked to recommend topics for future meetings. After looking at their suggestions, the coordinating team felt the most-needed topic was "Growing in Relationship: Implications for Family Life and Work." When the new sessions began, less than half the original group came. Curious because of the group's overwhelming request for follow-up sessions, the steering committee wrote the original members and asked why they dropped out of the group. Many answered that the topic was on target but, if they attended, certain hard questions would have to be asked, which might involve a change of family lifestyle or work activities. These participants were not ready to risk hearing God's word in the very concrete world of their daily lives.

This attitude is not new. History and anthropology tell of many civilizations that believed in a supreme god, a god with whom they were not concerned in everyday life, but one to whom they prayed in necessity. While times were good, these people forgot the supreme god, turning instead for intercession and protection to lesser gods dwelling in the hearth, trees, rocks and other places. Only in times of need did they return to the supreme god, sometimes called the sky god, for help and protection. Is it different today when lesser gods are often such things as money, pleasure and possessions?

It is something of a paradox to call the world a chief source of evangelization, because contemporary culture gives the opposite message. The economy is geared around money. Sex sells, youth sells, Christmas sells. In our culture, the Christmas season is the biggest sales event of the year, not a profound religious feast.

In the midst of this environment Catholic evangelization challenges people to look more deeply at the real purpose of money and work. These things are means to an end, instruments of God's kingdom, intended by God to help people build the earth into God's image of love, peace and compassion. God never intended the secular to be divorced from the sacred. This is a modern phenomenon. Ancient peoples saw human labor as necessary to survive, to maintain life — and all life was sacred. The primary emphasis was on relationships — family, tribe, friends; things were secondary. Possessions, warfare, emigration and religious devotions served family, tribe, friends and God. People attempted in this way to balance the ultimate and functional dimensions of life.

Unfortunately today many people minimize relationships and canonize things. The outcome of this attitude is bleak. People need ultimate responses to ultimate needs, for example, deep reciprocal love between spouses, parents and children. When people get functional responses to ultimate needs, for example, when a child receives a new suit or even a new toy instead of the affection needed from a parent, the result is alienation. Alienation abounds today. People who do not receive ultimate responses to ultimate needs hunger for something more, something deeper.

But the contemporary picture is not totally bleak, for within this environment voices cry out for justice and charity. They come from rich and poor, young and old. We hear them in supermarkets and classrooms. Sometimes this cry finds expression in social work and the helping professions. Other times people discover ways to evangelize within their particular environments. Recently Tricia, an engineering student, felt moved to change her major to social work. After considerable thought, she decided to remain in engineering, where she hoped to make a difference in the business world.

During the '60s, Jim, another student, discussed similar issues with me. His friends spent much of their time in inner city ministry. He was a math major and thought about switching to counseling. But he was getting all A's and he really loved math. I said, "Jim, perhaps God has blessed you with great math talents and calls you to be the best mathematician you can be as your life's work. Look at the people you will help if you advance humankind by your contributions!" Jim stayed in math, earned a master's degree and a Ph.D. Now he is a professor at a large state-run university, is on numerous national and international commissions, and applies his Christian values to his work. Jim is a corporate evangelist and affects decisions at a corporate level. This would not have been possible if he had become a counselor. His story invites people to respond to their

God-given gifts. The church's challenge is to help people clarify their calling, encouraging them to break down the sacred/secular dichotomy.

God invites people to influence the world and build it in light of God's kingdom. Another positive element today is the shrinking of our world into what some have called a "global village." The technology explosion — rapid communication, television, computers — has brought various races and ethnic peoples together and made people aware of human concerns across the world. This promises new opportunites for global evangelization. The world, in coming together, becomes more God-like.

Church

Church means any Christian community that gathers on a regular basis to profess belief in Jesus, engage in ritual worship and serve the kingdom. It includes groups such as parishes, Catholic schools, dioceses and religious communities. The Christian community discloses Jesus' message to family and world and illuminates the already-present activities of God. Great variety may exist in church groupings but certain basic elements are the same. Here we will look at these common elements and the way they relate to evangelization.

1. *The church roots all evangelizing activities in welcome and hospitality.*   Effective parishes are welcoming parishes. Welcome is not something one feels because a parish has greeters at Sunday Mass. Rather, welcome permeates a parish's style, spirit and vitality. This welcome extends beyond Sunday Mass to parish clubs, organizations and social gatherings. Hospitality is apparent in the way secretaries answer the door or phone, by the way custodians assist people seeking information, by the response a person gets when coming to the rectory, by the general parish attitude toward new parishioners.

Just as we know immediately whether we are welcome in a parish, we also know when we are not welcome. This inhospitable attitude is not always obvious to established community members.

"We've always done it this way" and "How dare a newcomer tell us what to do" are slogans that keep new people at a distance. It's hard to feel welcome in some church organizations. Often people who are long-time members of a parish are simply unaware of newcomers, since they are deeply involved in their own circle of family, friends and acquaintances. Years ago, my dad went to a meeting in a parish he joined the week before. After feeling isolated and neglected for an hour, while the others chatted and had fun, he left. Dad never went to another social gathering in that parish, although he attended liturgical functions there for many years.

Sometimes one's state in life or ethnic background makes a difference in the welcome a person receives. Single people often feel out of place at parish gatherings that are largely organized for parents and children. Blacks, Hispanics and members of other ethnic groups may not experience genuine hospitality. Parishes need to develop a sensitivity to such situations. In the same way, more can be done to welcome people of other faiths on occasions such as weddings, funerals or graduations.

Effective evangelization cannot happen when welcome is missing. It is central to Jesus' spirit of healing and forgiveness. When we feel welcome, we know God's kingdom is present.

2. *Church affords community support beyond the realm of family, friendships, work or civic associations.* We have seen that church groups must ground their evangelization efforts in qualities of welcome, support and affirmation. This is especially important today because contemporary people often find it hard to experience community, even among family and friends, due in large part to changes in family life and a highly mobile society. Civic meetings, sports groups, card clubs, fitness centers and work environments sometimes provide a point for connecting with people of similar interests but people are searching for an experience of community that goes beyond these rather superficial connections.

Church communities can provide this experience of transcendence, celebration, faith sharing and ultimate meaning. Church groups can help people understand what is happening in their lives in light of Jesus' message. But just as a parish or other church group needs to be genuinely welcoming, so too it needs to be a significant expression of community. When people perceive a parish as just another organization unable to meet their ultimate needs, they will not become active members. Often people say that the church is irrelevant to their lives. The message is not irrelevant, but many contemporary parishes communicate it in ways that are at best questionable.

Church evangelization does not depend on more organizational structures, finances, parish lists or computers. The post-Vatican II church, following "The Constitution on the Church in the Modern World," has entered into dialogue with society, using modern media, organizational development and business practices in church ministry. Unfortunately the church has often created large bureaucracies that demand big budgets, a new style of pastor-manager and offices not significantly different from secular businesses. What's happened to the kingdom of God in all this? Not long ago, a parish minister reluctantly shared this story.

A parish council meeting was ready to begin when the doorbell rang. A poorly dressed woman, known in the neighborhood as trying to make ends meet in a very painful family situation, asked to speak to the pastoral minister. Tears ran down her cheeks as she briefly told her sad story. The minister, anxious to get to the meeting, gave her a few moments, excused herself, and asked the woman to return the next day. At the meeting that night the parish talked about how to help the poor. Later the parish minister realized the irony of the situation. The woman never came back the next day.

To be sure, there are times when parish ministers cannot respond immediately to every request. But why is it today that few people show up at rectories or ministry centers unannounced? If they do, ministers may give them the impression, "Why are you bothering us? We've got work to do."

Do churches see the folly of planning to help the poor while not recognizing opportunities to help them every day? Evangelization must begin within church institutions themselves. Parishes, schools and religious communities need to live out the message of the kingdom, not play politics, build bigger buildings or arrange more meetings. Only in the context of the kingdom of God will a sense of community flourish in the church.

3. *Church becomes prophetic to family and world if prophecy is present within its organizational structures.* In the Judeo-Christian tradition, prophecy, "speaking for God," is rooted in the community. Yahweh called the Hebrews to be a prophetic people through their fidelity to Yahweh's call. When they deviated from this call, prophets like Isaiah, Ezekiel and Jeremiah called them back. The prophets constantly addressed the word of God to their current situation. Their voices radically opposed the established religious or social order when it was not in keeping with Yahweh's intentions.

Jesus' challenge to the unjust power of civic and religious institutions took shape in his message of forgiveness, healing and compassion. Jesus' prophetic mission is particularly clear when he exposes the false religiosity of the Pharisees and challenges them to return to the original spirit of Judaism.

Prophecy continues in the church community, where the risen Lord manifests his prophetic witness in the Christian assembly. The ministry of the word now incarnate in the church is prophetic. To prophesy is to proclaim the good news, to evangelize, to be converted by God's saving actions. All church members are called to witness to salvation by relating their stories to the kingdom of God that Jesus proclaimed. To bear witness to Christ in word or deed is to communicate God's prophetic word.

The institutional church influences the Christian community's vision of the Spirit's presence. The church's organizational structures can exercise powerful prophetic witness to Jesus' kingdom message by living and sharing Jesus' compassion, healing and forgiveness.

Prophecy can be incorporated into organizational structures of the church in two ways. The first incorporates the kingdom message into the institution itself. This means pastoral ministers, church associations and support staff live by a philosophy rooted in compassion, justice, forgiveness and healing. The following story illustrates a prophetic approach.

Last year, a sisters' community began its chapter meeting on a Sunday afternoon with the keynote address. As two sisters living near the motherhouse were getting into their car to go to the meeting, a small boy approached them, crying. The sisters recognized him as a child whose father died two months before. Jimmy told them how hard it was at home and asked if they would come to see his sick mom. The sisters went and never made it to the keynote. They chose people over meetings, incorporating the kingdom message into what they did. It would have been easy to say, "Sorry, Jimmy, we can't come now. We'll come over tomorrow." When the sisters arrived after the opening celebration, some sisters wondered why they had not been there. Maybe a few might have judged the meeting more important than little Jimmy. But as one of the sisters said, "I don't care what others think. Jimmy needed us."

It is a great challenge for parish ministers to incorporate this kingdom message into every facet of the parish. Some ways that this takes place include:

— Preferring people over meetings, structures and activities.

— Paying a just wage to employees. The salaries of many church employees, including parish ministers and Catholic school teachers, are unjust. The excuse that a person chooses to work for the church and should not expect much of a salary is not valid and cannot be justified when people need the money to live or raise a family.

— Putting priority on compassion, healing and forgiveness. When parish leaders are symbols of reconciliation, their example can evangelize the entire parish.

The second way the church incorporates the prophetic dimension is by challenging the community to justice and charity. It is important here to note that the church must distinguish between justice and charity. Recently in a midwest city gentrification of a poor neighborhood near the heart of the business district led to the displacement of many of the neighborhood's residents. After a poor, 85-year-old man was found near death in an alley, the incensed community raised cries of "We want justice, not charity." After a long process of re-examining the entire gentrification process, legislation was passed to protect the poor. But a Catholic activist involved in the struggle said the hardest group to deal with was her own church: "The church gives money each year to the poor (charity), but when it came to taking a stand for the poor (justice), and possibly stepping on the toes of influential church benefactors, the church hesitated." When this happens, little prophetic witness or evangelization happens. Jesus spoke a clear message of justice. He never worried about keeping influential people or groups happy. Church leaders can learn from his courageous example.

The effectiveness of the church's prophetic challenge to society depends on how the church itself lives out its prophetic calling. The United States bishops have spoken out for economic justice. But how prophetic is it to hold social action, catechetical or ministerial conventions with themes like "Justice and the Poor" at hotels where four-day meetings cost participants over $500, plus travel expenses, to attend?

Kingdom prophecy must be lived out by church ministers, for the church's way of doing things speaks eloquently about its real message. When both the message and the action witness to Jesus' message of compassion, healing and forgiveness, evangelization comes alive and people are saved.

FIVE

Catholic Evangelization: Word, Worship and Service

Even though the changes of Vatican II eliminated many traditional customs, we can discover an expression of church that is distinctively Catholic. We see this in interpretation of scripture, ecclesiology, hierarchical structure, ministry, sacraments and morality. This Catholic perspective underlies this chapter. We will consider word, worship and service as central aspects of the evangelization process and then suggest the main characteristics of Catholic evangelization.

Welcome, support and prophecy lay the foundation for Catholic evangelization in parishes, schools, religious communities, Catholic organizations, families and individual lives. Evangelization means more, however, and centers around a message to be taught, celebrated and lived.

Years ago while assisting in a parish I noticed a girl and two boys each Sunday in the front pew of church. No adult ever came with them. Lisa was about nine, her brothers six and four. Their poor clothes told me they came from a struggling family. I began to see the kids more and more in the school yard. The girl always showed up to help at the festival or bingo. I learned their parents were divorced, and the children lived with a grandmother. Lisa went to communion each week.

The week before Catechetical Sunday in September I announced that sign-up for religion classes for children attending public schools would be held after Mass. The parents were instructed to make the necessary arrangements. After Mass, I walked down the aisle toward the vestibule. Turning around, I saw the poorly dressed children following me. When I got to the back, Lisa, looking at her brother, blurted out anxiously, "Father, who will teach us about God?" Overcome with emotion, I put my arms around the children and hugged them.

Who will teach us about God? These words express the heart of evangelization. I sensed God's presence in Lisa and her brothers. In their simple way they lived Jesus' message. They also lived according to the central aspects of the evangelization process. Lisa taught her brothers what she knew of Jesus (word), celebrated God's presence with them at Mass (worship) and tried her best to support them and help around the parish (service). She was a remarkable nine-year-old girl.

This story invites Christians to reflect on Jesus, who came to proclaim a kingdom of love and service. All ministry is the ongoing communication of God's love for all people. This love is shared in the real presence of the death and resurrection of Jesus among us. Evangelization is the witness in word and deed that this is happening. Through the Christian community, the risen Christ invites people to transform their lives and follow him.

All Christians share in Jesus' mission to bring about God's kingdom. This mission has three aspects: to proclaim and teach God's word, to celebrate the sacred mysteries and to serve the people of the world. Three ministries serve this mission: word, worship and service. Even though we discuss them separately, these ministries cannot exist in isolation; each includes and implies the others.

In proclaiming the dying and rising of Jesus, evangelization energizes Christian endeavors, thereby reminding people of their mission to hasten God's kingdom. All ministry needs to be rooted in evangelization. Without it, individual or institutional efforts to proclaim the word, celebrate it or serve others lack the dynamism promised by the good news. An illustration shows the relationship between evangelization and the ministries that serve the mission of Christ and the church.

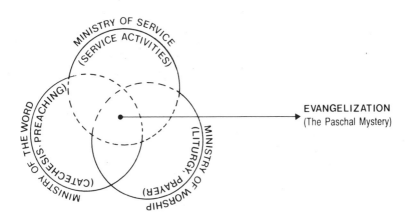

Evangelization is the energizing center of all Christian ministry. It provides the dynamism for the ministries of word, worship and service. The ministries of word, worship and service are inseparably linked and never exist in isolation, even though in a particular ministry or at a given time or place one or the other may predominate.

Evangelization in a community of word, worship and service constitutes the heart of the church's witness to the presence of Jesus. Effective evangelization, an ongoing activity of the

Christian community, requires keeping a healthy balance among the three ministries.

Word

Christianity is good news. To appreciate this message means discovering God's word in the Christian context. St. John's gospel begins:

> In the beginning was the Word;
> the Word was with God
> and the Word was God (Jn 1:1).

John goes on to describe the unfolding of God's revelation, centered in the Word, Jesus. Creation begins a process of God's self-revelation that climaxed in Jesus and continues through the church. The Christian community continues to proclaim the Word-made-flesh both sacramentally in the church and in various ministries that clarify God's salvific plan.

The ministry of the word in a pastoral context centers on manifesting the Judeo-Christian message in such ministries as preaching and catechesis.

Preaching

Many church members feel that they do not receive support, insight or wisdom from Catholic preaching. It does not help them appreciate how God's word applies to their lives. A sign of this dissatisfaction is a steady movement away from the Catholic church. Increasing numbers of people, especially in Hispanic communities, are joining fundamentalist churches.

Recently a Catholic pastoral minister received a letter from a family who had been very active in the parish. The letter thanked the minister for what the parish did for them. Then it continued, "Unfortunately, we were not fed by God's word. After much prayer we decided to join a Protestant church where the preaching, catechesis and scripture studies will give us what we never received in the Catholic church."

Biblical fundamentalism appeals to people in part because of its effective preaching. Fundamentalist preachers proclaim the scriptures in simple, straightforward, understandable language. In contrast, many people find Catholic preaching theoretical, complex or uninspiring.

Sunday Mass is the only time most people are exposed to the church. The homily is a spiritual lifeline to help people appreciate how God's word touches their daily activities. Every homilist cannot be a charismatic preacher, but every homilist must proclaim God's word in a prayerful, simple way. Effective preaching must relate the biblical message to people's needs. Preaching is not an exegetical session where the latest theories of biblical scholarship can be presented. It must, however, have the scriptures at its center. The focus of the reading is always God's word, Jesus' life. But this word must speak to people today — in their families, their jobs, their social life — and transform them into closer followers of Jesus. Preachers can gain valuable help in this by listening to what people are saying about their needs, their hopes, their struggles. They might also listen to what people say about how they hear God's word in their lives. The insight gained through such listening can then be proclaimed in a way that the whole community can identify with and respond to.

Catechesis

The journey of faith is lifelong. Catechesis, which is closely linked with a person's ongoing need for conversion, begins in childhood and lasts until death. The Rite of Christian Initiation emphasizes that coming to faith and deepening one's faith involve questioning, learning the good news, accepting membership in the Christian community and deepening the yes we make to Christ and the church throughout our lives (see the *Rite of Christian Initiation of Adults*, no. 4–40). Catechesis is the primary means by which we do this.

As a ministry of the word, "the definitive aim of catechesis is to put people not only in touch but in communion, in intimacy with Jesus Christ" (*Catechesis in Our Time*, no. 3). Catechesis refers to all efforts in the church "to make disciples, to help people to believe that Jesus is the Son of God, so that believing they might have life in his name, and to educate and instruct them in this life and thus build up the Body of Christ" (*Catechesis in Our Time*, no. 1). Catechesis, to accomplish its full purpose, must simultaneously strengthen individual faith and deepen involvement in the community. Catechesis helps families and parish communities to better appreciate and respond to the living Lord, whose presence is discerned in individual and communal experiences, in the scriptures and in church tradition.

Catechesis is a very important element in the evangelization process. Pope John Paul II, in *Catechesis in Our Time*, describes catechesis as a means of evangelization:

> Evangelization — which has the aim of bringing the good news to the whole of humanity, so that all may live by it — is a rich, complex and dynamic reality, made up of elements, or one could say moments, that are essential and different from each other, and that must all be kept in view simultaneously. Catechesis is one of these moments — a very remarkable one — in the whole process of evangelization (*Catechesis in Our Time*, no. 18).

The content of catechesis is identical to the content of evangelization, namely the person and gospel of Jesus Christ:

> Within the whole process of evangelization, the aim of catechesis is to be the teaching and maturation stage, that is to say, the period in which the Christian, having accepted by faith the person of Jesus Christ as the one Lord and having given him complete adherence by sincere conversion of heart, endeavors to know better this Jesus to whom he has entrusted himself: to know his "mystery," the kingdom of God proclaimed by him, the requirements and promises contained in his Gospel message, and the paths that he has laid down for anyone who wishes to follow him (*Catechesis in Our Time*, no. 20).

Catechesis can be viewed in two ways. "Informal" catechesis includes pastoral activities — family prayer, speaking of God's love to a friend, community building, evangelizing activities, service projects, liturgy — that have a catechetical aspect, even though their primary purpose is not to catechize. Many activities in the church's pastoral ministry have a catechetical aspect. These activities, rooted in the church's evangelical witness, provide a receptive climate for God's word, and prepare for or complement systematic catechesis. Pope John Paul II illustrates this when he says:

> While not being formally identified with them, catechesis is built on a number of elements of the Church's pastoral mission that have a catechetical aspect, that prepare for catechesis, or that spring from it. These elements are: the initial proclamation of the gospel or missionary preaching through the kerygma to arouse faith, apologetics or examination of the reasons for belief, experience of Christian living, celebration of the sacraments, integration into the ecclesial community, and apostolic and missionary witness (*Catechesis in Our Time*, no. 18).

For example, although the eucharistic celebration is explicitly a liturgical action, it has a catechetical aspect in the homily and prayers. In a similar way, when service projects are done in the spirit of the gospel, they are intimately related to the word of God.

Formal or "systematic" catechesis includes those pastoral activities that call forth a response to the living word of God in a deliberate, intentional and structured way. Systematic catechesis emphasizes understanding, reflection and transformation. It addresses the whole person and invites a change of one's life through listening and responding to God's word. Pope John Paul II describes systematic catechesis as a "matter of giving growth, at the level of knowledge and in life, to the seed of faith sown by the Holy Spirit with the initial proclamation and effectively transmitted by baptism" (*Catechesis in Our Time*, no. 20).

Systematic catechesis has "the twofold objective of maturing the initial faith and of educating the true disciple of Christ by means of a deeper and more systematic knowledge of the person and message of our Lord Jesus Christ" (*Catechesis in Our Time*, no. 19). In other words, systematic catechesis is didactic, that is, concerned about teaching the word to those ready to listen;

it also helps God's word to mature in the minds and hearts of those being catechized.

Systematic catechesis employs a definite methodology and aims at presenting the entirety of the Christian message in an orderly and sequential way. It "includes especially the teaching of Christian doctrine imparted, generally speaking, in an organic and systematic way, with a view to initiating the hearers into the fullness of Christian life" (*Catechesis in Our Time*, no. 18). This does not, however, imply a rigid structure for catechetical activities; rather, it refers to consciously planned and prepared catechetical efforts. Systematic catechesis may take place in classrooms, homes, retreat settings, or other parish or family surroundings, using varied approaches and processes.

The catechetical process is dynamic, ecclesial, interpersonal and biblical. It aims at deepening a person's faith and Christian life. The catechetical process may use different approaches or methods but it always includes four basic elements:

— *Human Experience*. Catechesis addresses a person in the context of his or her life and journey of faith — present needs, past experiences and future aspirations. Life experiences form the basis for listening and responding to God's word.

— *Message*. The catechetical process shows how the revealed message of the Hebrew and Christian scriptures, as well as the teachings of the church, shed light on a person's experience. Through methods such as storytelling, drama, scripture study, audiovisuals, lectures and discussions, this dimension of the catechetical process teaches and informs.

— *Reflection/Discovery/Integration*. After hearing the message proclaimed, a person needs to make it his or her own by asking the question, "How will this change my life if I accept and live it?" Through personal faith-sharing, group dynamics, journal-keeping, directed reflection, modern parables and value clarification techniques, people come to understand their feelings about the revealed message and to see its challenges and implications. This element of catechesis focuses on insight, internalizing the message and ongoing conversion.

— *Response*.   Finally, the catechetical process invites a personal response to God's word.   This leads to such acts of service and worship as volunteer service projects, prayer services, liturgical celebrations, creative expressions of the message in writing, art or music, and new resolutions for one's life.

The four elements in the catechetical process are interrelated, blending into a vibrant proclamation of the good news in the life of individuals and of the faith community itself.   Since catechesis happens in community as the risen Lord most often discloses himself to individuals through the faith of the church, each element of the catechetical process includes a communal as well as a personal response.

While the task of systematic catechesis is proclaiming the revealed message to people who have not heard it before, changing circumstances require that God's word be heard ever anew, especially by adults. Rooted in evangelization, catechesis continually invites people to probe more deeply into the mystery of God's love. "Catechesis is necessary both for the maturation of the faith of Christians and for their witness in the world" (*Catechesis in Our Time*, no. 25). It helps people face life's challenges out of a Christian perspective.

The ongoing task of catechesis is to foster mature faith. *Sharing the Light of Faith*, the National Catechetical Directory, stresses the importance of adult catechesis. It says, "Every form of catechesis is oriented in some way to the catechesis of adults, who are capable of a full response to God's word. Catechesis is a life-long process for the individual and a constant and concerted pastoral activity of the Christian community" (*Sharing the Light of Faith*, no. 32).

Worship

Preaching and catechesis sometimes take place in a ritual liturgical context. Worship, the second element in the evangelization process, includes liturgy and prayer. Christian worship praises and honors God and celebrates our redemption from sin and death. In other words, it celebrates the values from which faith springs.

For Christians, worship centers on the paschal mystery. Christian liturgy is the communal celebration of the ongoing dying and rising of Jesus by people who are called together in the Spirit to remember the continued gift of God's love, to engage in rituals that commemorate the paschal mystery and to respond in service to the permanent reality of God's Spirit.

While all liturgy acknowledges God's self-manifestation and the community's response in prayer, not all liturgical celebrations have the same focus or intensity. Tradition and the history of the community dictate the form of liturgical activities. The eucharistic liturgy, the seven sacraments or mysteries of the Christian life and the Liturgy of the Hours are the church's central liturgies. These public manifestations of the church's fullness employ official liturgical rites and are presided over by designated ministers. Family prayer, popular devotions and other communal prayers pertain to the liturgy, but celebrate the paschal mystery in a less comprehensive way.

The Rite of Christian Initiation of Adults ritualizes the dynamics inherent in the Christian journey toward the kingdom. It celebrates the dynamism of evangelization by emphasizing that the process whereby people are initiated ever more deeply into the mystery of Jesus' dying and rising happens within a faith community.

The church community, the basis of all evangelical activity, constantly initiates people into the conversion process. This process points to three community responsibilities. The first centers on a responsibility to active church members. Because conversion is lifelong, Christians must constantly grow together through catechesis, worship and service. The second responsibility directs the conversion process toward baptized Christians who either do not know or hardly appreciate the message of the church and God's love. The community invites them to grow in appreciation of the good news. The third responsibility is to initiate unbaptized people into the church. The community helps them discover whether the Lord is inviting them to follow him by becoming members of the church community and helps them respond to this call.

Evangelization and conversion — each centered on the paschal mystery — are integral aspects of one process by which a person comes to and grows in faith. Conversion includes both individual and ecclesial elements. It embraces the totality of a person's intellectual, moral and religious growth. The RCIA ritualizes ongoing Christian conversion, expressing the ministry of worship through a celebration of hearing God's word and responding in Christian service.

Service

Evangelization proclaims a kingdom of service. Jesus came as one who served, and the church continues this ministry. Every Christian is called to serve. Service includes efforts to provide a loving, Christian atmosphere at home, a listening ear when a colleague is troubled and any ministry in the marketplace that is motivated by kingdom values. Many church-related activities, from professional ministry to volunteer work, including St. Vincent de Paul, Legion of Mary and Daughters of Charity, are service. A high school student serves by helping in a nursing home; an older adult serves by giving advice to a grandchild. Service is illustrated in the following story from my childhood.

When I was a boy, an old black man named Ezra daily pushed a small cart up the street next to our store. His back was bent, but his eyes sparkled whenever he called out, "Rags, old iron!" in a garbled chant. In the summer people bought ice for their ice boxes and sold him old rags and pieces of scrap iron.

As he worked, children often danced around his cart, asking for a piece of ice to cool the heat of the summer. He took his ice pick, cracked off a corner, gave it to the children and told them to be good.

In the winter coal replaced the ice, and his chant became "Coal, coal!" as he sold small blocks of coal to help heat the homes in this poor area.

When he got tired, he sometimes sat in the store with my dad. I never spoke to him, but I admired his goodness and smile.

Each year around Christmas he came into the store and poured a bag of money on the counter. Ezra always said, "Mr. Hater, will you count it? How much can I buy this year?" Then Dad told him to pick out what he needed. Before I got wise, I wondered why Dad always said he had enough money for whatever items he put on the counter. One year I thought, "How can those few coins pay for all that merchandise?" His choice of merchandise baffled me. He always selected children's items — shoes, blouses, dresses, socks, underwear, pants, shirts and toys. Then he and Dad talked and wished each other a Merry Christmas.

One year when I reached high school age, I asked Dad about Ezra. "He is a wonderful old man, Bob," Dad said. I replied, "He sure must have a lot of children since he buys so much kids' stuff!" Dad smiled, continuing, "You don't know who he is, do you, Bob?" I said, "Yes, Dad, he is the ice and coal man." Dad went on, "There is more to Ezra. Ezra is the preacher at the small store-front church down on Poplar Street. The church has about 20 adult members. He buys presents for the children in his congregation. Ezra hasn't much education, but I know one thing: His congregation learns God's love from him. He knows the Bible and lives it, even when he sells ice and coal. Ezra is a real Christian."

When I think of service as a focal point of evangelization, I remember Ezra. His life taught me the meaning of Christian service. I never attended his church, but if his congregation followed his example, they could have been described like the early Christian gatherings: "They come together, tell the old, old, story, break bread, and go out and live the message they heard."

Characteristics of Catholic Evangelization

Catholic evangelization is based in creation, in the life of Jesus, in the kingdom of God and in the church community. This section summarizes the primary characteristics of Catholic evangelization.

Radically Incarnational

Evangelization is rooted in creation and happens in the midst of everyday life. God communicates through creation, sunsets, mountains, birds, plants and people.

Family, world and church are the primary disclosure points of Christian evangelization. Evangelization begins in a Christian family as people learn life's meaning through the joys and struggles of everyday living. The world of friends, society, work, science, neighbors, technology and business is often another fruitful place to discover God's presence or share Jesus' message.

The church communicates Jesus' mission under the guidance of the magisterium. A parish, diocese or religious community gathers God's people to hear the word, celebrate it and respond to it by serving others. The Christian community discloses Jesus' message to family and world by illuminating the presence of God already at work in them. When family, world and church are partners in evangelization, God's presence is communicated fully.

Community Directed

Catholic evangelization is centered in community, not in a "me and Jesus" experience. From our earliest years, we discover God through people. Catholic belief teaches that we are called as "a people" to follow Jesus, who himself called a community of disciples. Evangelization's first witness comes through community, usually family. We seek a personal relationship with God in union with, not in isolation from, our brothers and sisters in faith. Evangelization that stresses personal conversion and does not account for the community faith dimension is one-sided and incomplete.

Ecclesially Balanced

Catholic evangelization sees God's Spirit active in a healthy dialogue between the whole church community and the hierarchy. This balance insures that dynamic gospel values and authentic church teaching will be maintained. Christianity has never been a "believe in what you want" religion. Early in the Christian era, the apostles and bishops, entrusted with the preservation of Jesus' authentic message, guided the entire church community when heresies and false teachings emerged.

Catholic evangelization stresses this balance today. Prophets and teachers minister throughout the body of believers, under the guidance of the magisterium. Balanced dialogue within the entire church community guarantees fidelity to God's revelation and avoids the one-sided interpretations that sometimes characterize evangelists who center on a "me and Jesus" individual conversion.

Biblically Comprehensive

The Christian scriptures emerged from early community belief and represent the earliest church interpretations of Jesus' words and deeds. The scriptures are community faith statements, written with a definite purpose and literary form. Some were literal accounts; others were not. Literal interpretations of every passage are inadequate and at times in error. God's word was revealed through human expressions that varied according to time, place and literary style. It makes no more sense to insist on a literal interpretation of every scriptural account than to demand the same literal interpretation of a newspaper's news articles, editorials and comics.

While Catholic evangelization insists that all scripture is God's word, it demands comprehensive biblical interpretation, taking into account the various factors that influenced a given text. We understand a passage's meaning most fully when it is interpreted according to the reason it was written, the community that formed its primary audience and the literary form in which it was written. Since this in not always clear, guidance comes from church tradition, magisterial teaching and scholarly research.

Although the Catholic tradition insists on the authority of the church in biblical interpretation, we are encouraged to study scripture, pray with it and allow its message to touch the personal aspects of our lives, teaching us as individuals how God speaks.

Kingdom Centered

The goal of Catholic evangelization is the kingdom of God proclaimed by Jesus, which centers on reconciling and healing people whose lives are broken economically, physically, psychologically and spiritually. Catholic evangelization never loses sight of the kingdom's movement in the ordinary affairs of life.

To say that the primary goal of Catholic evangelization is to "make new church members" is narrow and one-sided. It leads to unfortunate proselytization. We should invite others into our Catholic community, but we must remember that the Roman Catholic Church is one way, not the only way, to disclose God's kingdom.

Catholic evangelization sees reconciliation and ministry to broken people as signs of living in God's kingdom. It rejects evangelistic efforts that regard material success, wealth or miraculous healings as signs of righteousness or of God's special favor.

Dynamically Holistic

Rooted in God's kingdom, Catholic evangelization energizes a community to proclaim the living Christ through the ministries of word, worship and service. All church organizations, structures and programs exist to help the community evangelize through the ministry of the entire church.

These ministries merge at many points and cannot function effectively in isolation. Catechesis, liturgy and social action may overlap in their expressions, even though they are primarily centered in the ministries of word, worship and service, respectively.

Catholic evangelization is one process with many aspects. Proclaiming God's word is integrally related to prayer, Eucharist, community worship and social concern. Catholic evangelization efforts flow from the paschal mystery and are unified in a holistic vision of God's word, experienced and celebrated in a vibrant faith life.

Optimistic but Realistic

Catholic evangelization believes the world is basically good, but admits the presence of sin. God created a good world and people are fundamentally good but sin disrupts this harmony. The creation stories in Genesis account for the origins of sin and evil but also promise salvation. Catholic tradition teaches that after the Fall creation remained good but wounded. Catholics acknowledge a holy God guiding a good world and a Redeemer alive in the Christian community.

Catholic evangelization rejects fundamentalist preaching that says creation after the Fall is evil. This approach concentrates on sin and corruption and minimizes basic human goodness. While admitting sin's allurement and power, Catholic evangelization focuses on God's grace, which promises hope and freedom. God encourages people to turn from sin, repent and be reconciled. Human beings need God because the world is imperfect — people sin and every individual requires healing.

Process Oriented

Some forms of evangelism stress conversion as an "event" — a moment when one definitively says, "I'm saved!" Catholic evangelization holds that conversion is a continuous, lifelong process, even though one particular event such as sickness, death or a joyous occasion may trigger or intensify the conversion process. Evangelization is the ongoing effort of a pilgrim people to discover the mystery of God's kingdom on earth as they journey through life to the final realization of God's kingdom in heaven. In this process, faith and good works are necessary for salvation.

Integral to People's Lives

The evangelizing community begins by creating an atmosphere where rich, poor, young, old, divorced, single, healthy, hurting, Black, white and alienated people feel welcome. Evangelization begins when people are "at home." That's where they discover God. Then, following Jesus' lead, the Catholic evangelizer helps people see the significance of God's word in their lives. While insisting on the unchanging nature of God's word, Catholic evangelization stresses the constant need to apply it to people's lives. Scripture can illuminate human experiences and give new insights.

Consistently Directive

Catholic evangelization is stable and consistent, not shifting with the latest fad or whim. Rooted in a two-thousand-year tradition, it is ever fresh because of the Spirit's constant call to apply God's word to an ever-changing world. This means maintaining the "basics" while being open to personal and cultural changes.

The Catholic evangelizer helps people discover the real "fundamentals" of faith and encourages them to retain these basic beliefs as a constant guide to action. The consistently directive character of Catholic evangelization sees God's word as the cardinal motive, leading people to appreciate the meaning of life and the mystery of God's presence.

"Balanced" is the single word that summarizes Catholic evangelization: balanced among family, world and church; balanced among the ministries of word, worship and service. This balance begins with God, continues through Jesus and invites the church to holiness and wholeness.

SIX

Evangelization and Conversion

When we discover the Lord's life in the testimony of other people, it can become a powerful reflection on the meaning of faith. We see things in a new way and this new vision is the heart of conversion. Catholic evangelization invites us to pattern our lives after Jesus. A recent experience helped me to see this aspect of evangelization more clearly.

Last spring I went to a folk festival where booths of arts and crafts extended for two city blocks. In one booth, I spotted a beautiful painting of a thin old man with a wrinkled face and sun-dried hands, dressed in work clothes and holding a wooden mallet poised and ready to crack a shingle from a block of oak. Something about the old man captivated me.

As I stood gazing at the picture, the booth keeper said, "It's really something, isn't it? The price is also something — four thousand dollars. A local artist painted it. The shinglecracker lives near here. In fact, you can watch him crack shingles in a booth just over that hill to the right of my booth."

Interested in meeting the shinglecracker, I walked up the next line and found him speaking to a small boy and his father. On one side of his booth were several hundred cracked shingles; behind them stood large oak tree trunks, cut into pieces the length of a wooden roof shingle. At the other end of the booth the shinglecracker showed the boy how to crack a shingle.

The old man impressed me more than the picture. His worn hands revealed two knuckles missing, possibly from a past accident with the mallet and wedge. He put the wedge on the oak trunk, then struck it with the mallet, and the shingle split.

After the boy and his father left, I spoke with the shinglecracker. After a while he said, "Did you see my picture?" When I said I had, he continued, "Yesterday after they put it up, I went over and stood in back of the booth. Many people admired it. When I heard their kind words, I tapped one fellow on the shoulder and said, 'The copy is great, but turn around and look at the original. It's better.' It was nice to see their smiles as they looked at me."

I thought about how much they were charging for the painting, which wouldn't have been possible without the original to portray. It struck me how often people look at the copy and never get to the original. Soon my thoughts turned to faith. Humans, made in God's image, are beautiful copies of a divine image. Their beauty, however, fades when they fail to mirror the original. It is never enough to stop with the copy, no matter how splendid. To appreciate life one must return to the original and let this image shine. For Christians, the original is Jesus. Only in living by his example, given to us in the gospels, can we discover life's meaning.

Evangelization demands that we look at the original, Jesus Christ, and pattern our lives after him. In doing so we gradually become the original. As St. Paul says, "I live now not with my own life but with the life of Christ who lives in me" (Gal 2:20). This is the heart of life and the basis of Christian spirituality.

In this chapter we will look at evangelization and conversion. We will examine dimensions of God's revealing presence, the meaning of conversion, kinds of conversion, methods to facilitate conversion and practical questions.

Modes of God's Revealing Presence

Evangelization begins with God seeking people. This divine quest comes from within a person, is revealed through communities and is clarified through reflection. We can identify three dimensions or modes of this divine movement toward conversion, namely core, community and consideration modes. God gives life to one's spirit (core). This movement flows through group response (community), where family, friends and culture help shape attitudes and values. Finally, the outer limit of consciousness (consideration) reflects on the rational expression and implications of the revelation.

These modes can be compared to the flame of a candle. God lights the flame of revelation, and the world (the candle) sustains it through the divine energy present in life itself. The hottest part of the flame, the inner core, burns with the greatest intensity and represents our inner depths, where our deepest concerns lie. The outermost part of the flame, not as intense as the core, represents our intellectual or rational activity. The air that provides the oxygen necessary to sustain the candle may be compared to the community, which allows a person to grow.

Core

The core refers to a person's deepest dimension, where God's Spirit from within urges one to search for meaning. This wellspring, continually energized by God, roots life's meaning. Here people meet God in the form of spiritual energy, creative awareness and intuitive insight. From this source, questions such as "Who am I?" and "Why was I born?" emerge spontaneously. The whole person — body, emotions, reason, intuition and spirit — responds at this mode. A response that is excessively emotional or excessively rational does not genuinely manifest a core response.

This mode allows people of different religious beliefs to identify with someone else's deep story or personal experience. At a Hindu-Christian prayer service recently, when a Christian read a scripture account of Jesus' agony and death, the Hindu holy men wept, feeling deeply the universal meaning of sin, suffering and death.

Community

Community here describes interactions among people in family, world and church groups. People are influenced by the way a particular community interprets the energies flowing from the core mode. Cultural, historical and confessional beliefs affect the focus of one's deep core energies. No one can predict when, where and how God will be revealed. But since God is revealed in time, people's beliefs are influenced by different cultures. Consequently, believing Christians respond to Jesus' story from a core depth common to all religious people as well as from their particular customs and beliefs.

Consideration

When people reflect on their actions and beliefs, they operate in a consideration mode. This enables religious communities to formulate doctrines and creeds, as well as to understand motives for action. For example, after Jesus' death the Christian community struggled for centuries to clarify the precise relationship between Jesus' divinity and his humanity. The same clarification process happens today as the church attempts to address Jesus' message to an ever-changing global world. This mode also allows human beings to pass records on to succeeding generations, to interpret historical events and to develop models in science and theology. Models play an important role in clarifying issues. In a similar way an individual, after a significant experience, may rationally probe the motivation behind his or her actions. Reflection is integral to human learning.

All community conversion efforts seek to touch the dimension of mystery at the core, which roots the reflection that occurs.

These three modes are essential in the evangelization process, the ultimate goal of which is to link the person more deeply with God.

Meaning of Conversion

Before Vatican II, most Catholics used the term *conversion* to refer to people called "converts" who joined the church. Today Christian conversion focuses on a growing relationship with Jesus and the kingdom of God, with the church serving as an important element in this relationship. Conversion happens when people respond affirmatively to the evangelization process.

In a Christian context, conversion is a significant deepening, recentering or refocusing of one's attitudes, values, life patterns, energies and loyalties, as these relate to God, community and gospel values. Put simply, conversion is seeing and acting in a new way. This can happen in an individual's life, or it may involve a community (parish, family, friends).

Incentives for conversion come from nature, people, society and church. Since evangelization is the invitation and conversion the response, conversion, like evangelization, can be implicit or explicit. *Implicit* conversion means developing positive attitudes toward life or changing one's outlook as a result of an ongoing dialogue with life, with no explicit reference to God.

When I was a small boy, two events significantly affected my general outlook. The first happened when I was in the first grade. I became sick, and the doctor said I had to stay away from school for three months. For many children this would have meant repeating the first grade. But my mother taught me. Every day she spent hour after hour showing me how to spell, read, write and add. Her goodness, patience and love gave me confidence. Mom often walked to school, talked to the teacher, then taught me. When I returned to school, I was ahead of the rest of the class.

The second event happened three years later. During World War II a group of neighbors planted victory gardens in the empty lot behind our home. A successful businessman living up the street who grew up on a farm befriended me and taught me to prune tomatoes, grow pole beans, hoe radishes and prepare the soil for planting.

An old man named Sam had a patch of tomato plants at the end of the field where the soil was rocky. Every day he watered his plants, tried to hoe them and waited for tomatoes. But only small green ones appeared on the vines, soon withering from lack of nourishment. The old man kept watching for red tomatoes. His eyesight was not good, and sometimes I tried to help him find red tomatoes on his plants.

One day my businessman friend said, "Bob, we are going to assist nature and make old Sam happy. Only a miracle will put ripe tomatoes on his plants. So we'll make this miracle happen."

He took some nice red tomatoes from his garden but left about two inches of green stem on each tomato. Then we went to old Sam's patch and tied the ripe tomatoes on Sam's plants with very thin green thread.

When Sam discovered the ripe tomatoes, he called me over and said, "I'm satisfied now because I have ripe tomatoes."

My businessman friend professed no religion, but somehow what he did for old Sam stuck with me and revealed another facet of human responsibility.

As I grew, experiences like these, coming from God's presence in life itself, influenced me. Reactions to such events involve implicit conversion.

Explicit conversion implies acknowledgment that God breaks into human consciousness. This, too, comes gradually. During the months I stayed home from school, Mom taught me about God's love and support in my sickness. She showed me how to pray. Slowly the implicit conversion I learned from her goodness became more explicit as I sensed God's presence healing me. In the same way, years after the victory garden experience of tying tomatoes on Sam's stalks, I learned that God helps people as we helped Sam. The gardening experience eventually taught me to see God's all-encompassing providence. The early experience of implicit conversion became explicit, when I connected these childhood events with God.

Conversion is lifelong and ongoing. Experiences are constantly reintegrated into a person's personality as one deepens, shifts or changes life's priorities. Events will have varying degrees of significance, but God is present in the entire process. In this light, Christian conversion means taking on the mind and heart of Jesus in coming to appreciate life's meaning.

Kinds of Conversion

People come to conversion in different ways. Although conversion occurs in the complex web of life, we can identify two ways that conversion happens, namely, gradual and radical conversion.

Gradual conversion happens in life's give and take from childhood to old age. Most people come to God in this way and identify no single event as a definitive moment of conversion.

Radical conversion happens when a person can point to a definite experience that dramatically altered his or her life direction. For example, Jim had no active faith, though he was raised a Catholic. Then his child developed a rare disease that immobilized her. This changed Jim's outlook, and he became a devout believer who impressed others by the way he cared for his child. His child's sickness deeply changed him. Sometimes these traumatic experiences challenge one's faith or even lead to its denial. For example, one woman never attended church again after her child's sudden death. Previously this woman went to Mass every day.

Conversion is never one-sided; radical and gradual conversion happen together. The gradual process of conversion is affected by radical events that may force a person to change focus, and even with radical conversion the process is ongoing, as an individual gradually integrates a radical experience into the overall framework of his or her life.

The conversion process can be seen in the following illustration. You can probably draw a similar conversion pattern for your own life.

The Conversion Process

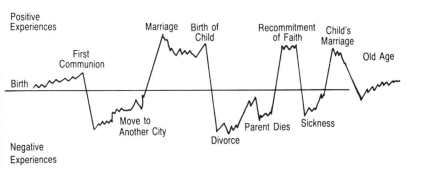

Conversion's goal is life, freedom, wholeness and health, which cannot be realized fully on earth. As St. Augustine said, "Our hearts are restless and they cannot rest until they rest in you, O God." The journey to God has many ups and downs. These peak and valley experiences jar people into a deeper realization of life's ultimate purpose and can trigger implicit or explicit conversion experiences.

Conversion has many faces. One that changed my life happened in the simplest way.

Once after a retreat I spent a day in silence and recollection. My life was going well; there were pressures, concerns and irritations but for the most part I felt happy and joyous. I went to bed late that night. Early the next morning, while beginning to wake up, I was overcome with a powerful experience. It seemed like the heart of conversion. Immediately I arose and jotted an expression on a piece of torn paper in order to remember the experience. Had I not, the event would have been lost. I wrote:

This morning I came to an awareness that I was being touched by a reality so deep that my whole inner self became suffused with meaning.

The goal of conversion is to touch one's inner core with meaning. This realization comes from God, for God alone gives meaning to life. All created life prepares for this divine-human encounter.

Four elements are common to the Christian conversion process: 1) personal experience; 2) situating that experience within a broader environment, such as the Judeo-Christian story; 3) illuminating the experience through this encounter with community by grounding it in prayer, scripture, church teaching and history; 4) responding to the insights gleaned from prayer, celebration and service. These four elements need not flow sequentially or be present at all times. They can occur in both individual and communal experiences of conversion.

Individual conversion refers to one person's unique faith journey to God. *Communal* conversion happens when a group (family, religious community, parish, RCIA group) moves together to a deeper appreciation of the journey of faith. Communal and individual conversions are interconnected.

Methods to Facilitate Conversion

Conversion helps people gain insight into life's meaning. In a sacramental, incarnational world, the search for meaning always returns to the core mode, where God intimately addresses people. To facilitate conversion we must acknowledge the core level out of which people respond.

While efforts to facilitate individual conversion center around shared meaning, a person's relationship with God roots all shared meaning. Individual conversion is always a personal search and ought to be facilitated as such. Nevertheless, community is central to conversion. In community, God is disclosed; in community, a person is supported and encouraged; in community, personal meaning is most fully revealed. It is important to keep the individual and communal aspects of conversion in a healthy balance.

The world in which God invites people to new levels of awareness includes three chief disclosure points: family, ecclesial community and personal activities such as work, prayer, play, friends, community involvement and nature. Facilitating conversion means acknowledging these disclosure points, seeing God's presence there, and developing methodologies consistent with a heterogeneous mix of people.

It is important to appreciate the difference between the *conversion process* itself and *methods* used to facilitate it. The ultimate purpose of individual or communal conversion is deeper union with God, achieved through relationships with the sacramental world. Individuals relate differently to communal beliefs and practices. Acknowledging unity in diversity yet diversity in community reinforces the need for flexible methodologies as people move across the boundaries of age, group, parish and country. While ultimate questions are the same for all people, their responses in community vary greatly due to local circumstances and group differences.

Many Methods

Every effort to facilitate conversion (for example, evangelization, catechesis, group sharing or liturgical celebrations) is a method or learning process. In catechesis, for example, methods may vary from lectures to group discussions. A method is valuable if it helps a person to discover God present within an experience and to reflect upon life in light of the Christian story, so as to move toward some life response, such as repentance, prayer, social action or charity. Different methods can be used at different phases of the conversion process. Effective methods take into account the person, the environment and the facilitator's gifts. There is no one best method to facilitate conversion or learning.

We can see an example of this if we look at the way conversion can happen in family settings. In informal settings, such as in families or with friends, the methods used to facilitate conversion need to be flexible. Family prayer may need to shift focus as children grow. Prayer groups may vary methods to accommodate the needs of individual members.

The process whereby families grow together in faith usually happens spontaneously. Birthdays, religious feasts and special events are celebrated. Kindness, patience, understanding, forgiveness and love cement family ties and bring ongoing conversion to the family community. Formal methods to assist the conversion process, like teaching children the Our Father or celebrating with an Advent wreath, complement the deeper conversion happening through family relationships.

Methods, however, are secondary to conversion itself. For example, saying the family rosary after dinner may be a more useful method in one situation (or with certain family members) than in another. Sunday liturgy is another key example. All family members should be encouraged to attend. But if a teenager refuses to go, a parent might, after a serious discussion with the teen, conclude that he or she is not lazy or making excuses, but really has faith problems. Forcing the youth to attend could possibly do more harm than good. A better approach might be for the parent to help the young person grow in faith (conversion) by discussing scripture and applying its message to the teenager's life. In turn, this may lead to a growing appreciation of the Mass. Here, conversion is facilitated by employing a method that relates to the current situation of the young person.

Selecting a Method

Since there are many methods to facilitate conversion, selecting a method depends on the people involved. In one instance, it may be wise to begin with a dialogue; in another, with a didactic approach, gradually moving to a collaborative one. No one method works at all times or with all people.

Conversion differs from person to person. Someone may wish to spend time alone to enhance conversion. Later, he or she may prefer limited group interaction or more intense dialogue. The person's preferences significantly influence the most appropriate method.

Because the individual's attitude significantly influences the conversion process, methodology and content materials should touch the experiences of the person or group. People's divergent attitudes also indicate why any systematic approach to conversion needs to move beyond community and consideration modes to the core mode.

On the level of communal conversion, it helps to distinguish natural groups (for example, separated and divorced people, children who have lost a parent) from more random groups (for example, a youth catechetical group or an adult enrichment program). A common concern binds together natural groups; random groups usually do not have the same binding force.

In addition to the people involved in the conversion process, the facilitator's style will also influence the method used. Some people are good group facilitators; others are more successful using a modified lecture format. All facilitators cannot be required to use the same technique if the process is to be effective. For example, not all religion teachers can use the same teaching method or textbook.

In the parish, distinguishing conversion itself from the methods used to facilitate it is helpful when considering the Rite of Christian Initiation of Adults. The RCIA advocates a flexible process, accommodated to personal needs and local circumstances. If the rite itself or a particular way of doing it is canonized, conversion may be blocked rather than facilitated.

Several examples illustrate this point. Today the ordinary way of fostering ecclesial conversion is through a catechumenal group. In one parish, however, a person interested in becoming a Catholic was sent to another parish because the person was not willing to join the parish catechumenal group. This is a question of methodology. Opportunities for participating in a modified catechumenate, including private instructions, should be provided to meet the needs of individuals. The goal is conversion, which can happen with or without the ordinary RCIA catechumenal process.

A second example pertains to using the lectionary readings as a catechetical method. Some parishes concentrate exclusively on these texts and use no other books, claiming this is the way it should be done to be faithful to the RCIA's origin and purpose. The origins of the catechumenate, however, reveal something else, namely, different methodologies developed in various churches (Rome, Jerusalem, Hippo, Constantinople, Milan) to prepare catechumens.

No universally accepted pattern of catechetical methodology is evident in the early history of the catechumenate. As the catechumenate developed, the Sunday Liturgy of the Word played a primary, but not exclusive, part in the content of catechetical instructions. In addition, catechetical and formational experiences sometimes happened in conjunction with the Liturgy of the Hours or at other times, often emphasizing the Creed. Most local churches followed a manner of instruction that shifted focus as catechumens moved from the initial stage of becoming catechumens, through the time immediately preceding baptism, to the postbaptismal catechesis. The method of catechesis was not the same in all churches. Instructions varied in approach and focus, apparently adapted to the bishop, ministers, place and people.

Historical data confirms the need to remain flexible in both the content and in the method used in the RCIA. Consequently, to claim that catechesis in the RCIA should be limited to reflections on the Sunday lectionary readings absolutizes a method, whereas in reality, lectionary readings are only one important means to facilitate conversion.

A final example pertains to catechesis. Here methods will also vary. To say that group sharing must happen in every instance is just as problematic as to insist that a lecture or storytelling always must precede group sharing. Whenever a method to facilitate conversion is absolutized, as often happened with the pre-Vatican II catechism method, the complexity of a person's conversion process can be lost. The method becomes more important than the person.

Consequently, if a method works for one group and facilitator, leading people to deeper faith, better appreciation of community and more profound links with God, who can say that another method would be better? The bottom line is conversion, not method.

The one common center upon which all conversion processes converge, and on which all methodologies focus, is every person's search for meaning and for God in the midst of a broken world. Jesus came to proclaim forgiveness, healing and reconciliation. We all experience some kind of brokenness in our lives. This common bonding provides the starting point for all efforts to facilitate conversion, efforts that ultimately focus on the core mode, where God alone can make a person whole.

Practical Questions

Systematic efforts to facilitate conversion aim at deepening people's relationships with God. To accomplish this, several questions should be asked.

1. Do the efforts to facilitate conversion recognize the difference between the conversion process itself, which is lifelong, and the various methods intended to help facilitate this process?

2. Does the method address the needs of the whole person? God's evangelizing action happens in the whole person — body, emotions, mind and spirit. Every method must integrate and balance all of these aspects.

3. Is it best to use a method that begins with personal sharing, or one that presents general information, followed by sharing that connects people's individual experiences with the common story? This question has no simple answer. It depends on the situation, time, facilitator and group. There is no one method for all occasions.

4. Is the method adequate, considering the age of the people with whom it is used? Several factors might be considered. The attention span of small children differs from that of adults. Children learn rituals; adolescents and adults search for the meaning of rituals. Adults have a rich font of experience; children do not. A method that works

well with one age group may not be as effective with people of another age.

5. Does the method provide an opportunity for the individual or group to grow in faith and be motivated to action? Renewal movements, such as Cursillo and charismatic groups, attempt to do this by connecting individuals to a larger community and providing support or nourishment for their actions.

Today's complex world invites Christians to return to the simple message of the gospels and to evangelize in a holistic way. This means recognizing the diversity of people and being realistic about community in our time. To proclaim the good news, no single methodology is sufficient. Methods need to be flexible in order to respond to personal and group needs. Christian ministers do well to look at how Jesus taught: He shared a message, told a story and invited people to consider its consequences and to derive meaning from the mystery of God-among-us. Jesus gave this challenge to his first disciples; he also gives it today.

SEVEN

Evangelization and Ministry

Evangelization is the heart of ministry. Church members need to develop a deeper appreciation of evangelization's challenge in family life, social activities, work and parish ministry. Jesus' mission was to proclaim the good news of the kingdom of God. He invited people to share this message. Evangelization, which continues Jesus' mission, centers around inviting people to share the Christian faith. Just as Jesus carried out his mission by his life (being) and deeds (doing), so do Christians, by inviting others to share God's love in the church community. This was brought home to me early in my priesthood.

Ellie, a parishioner, brought an elderly couple to Mass each Sunday. After seeing them for about two years, I asked her one Sunday about her friends. The four of us had spoken, but I didn't know the couple's background. Ellie said the man was Catholic, while his wife professed no religion.

I was impressed by this woman's sincerity, so I suggested that Ellie ask her some time if she ever thought about becoming a Catholic.

Several weeks later Ellie called me. She was overjoyed. When she asked her friend, the woman answered, "Thank you, I've been waiting 40 years for someone to invite me to be a Catholic."

This story illustrates the heart of evangelization — inviting others in word and deed to share Jesus' message in a Christian community. This can happen in the simplest ways — in families, among friends and at work. When centered on the kingdom of God, Christian response carries on Jesus' work, for just as Jesus' ministry fulfilled his mission, so the church's ministry carries out its mission of evangelization. Evangelization is not a separate ministry, but central to all ministry.

Ministry includes all intentional acts performed by Christians (individually or collectively) for the sake of the kingdom. Some people use the term *ministry* in a wide sense, analogous to the expression "Christian service." Seen in this way, ministry is equivalent to "Christian discipleship." Others restrict ministry to designated church service, for example, the work of an ordained priest, a pastoral associate or a religious education director. Relating ministry to evangelization need not get into these semantic issues, for no matter how the term is used, evangelization is the goal of all Christian activities.

Ministry in Perspective

The vision that sees ministry as rooted in every Christian's baptismal calling meshes with the holistic view of evangelization. The intentional activities performed by Christians for the sake of the kingdom carry out the Christian's call to evangelize. This call takes an individual beyond self to the broader society.

Every Christian is called to minister, but not all activity of baptized people is ministry. To qualify as ministry, human endeavors must be performed for the sake of the kingdom. An individual must explicitly or implicitly intend to fulfill the Christian calling to serve God's kingdom. A mother's family activities, for example, are ministry when she carries out her work to fulfill her Christian calling as a mother. She can explicitly make this intention, or implicitly do so.

Viewing ministry this way reminds one of the custom, once strongly recommended in the Catholic church, of saying the morning offering, thereby intending to give one's whole day to God for Christian service. By intending to offer daily work, parish service, neighborhood outreach or school activities for the sake of the kingdom, these actions become Christian ministry.

When Christians live their lives for the sake of the kingdom, family, marketplace (work), society in general, and church (parish) are focal points of ministry. In each sector, the already-present God invites Christian disciples to share the kingdom message by their lives, deeds and words.

Christians fulfill their vocations according to their gifts and responsibilities. Whatever the specific form of this calling, Christian ministry is energized by the ultimate evangelizing goal of all ministry — to share Jesus' kingdom message.

While ministry is not the exclusive domain of explicit church activities, all individual ministry must be linked in some way to the broader ecclesial community. Without this link, distortions can happen, as evidenced in the following story.

A Catholic high school student said her religion teacher did not believe Jesus was God. He spoke often about Jesus being a good man, a friend to follow, but did not believe that Jesus was divine, nor that he was present in the Eucharist. This teacher, once a strict Catholic, went through a rebellious phase, alienated himself from the institutional church, but still remained active in social causes. His teaching changed as he changed. When it became clear to school officials what he taught, he was treated fairly, but replaced.

The teacher in question was teaching "his own thing," not consistent with the believing community. Consequently, he did not qualify as a "Christian minister," for his humanistic perspective on Christ did not mesh with Christian tradition.

A minister is bonded to the larger church community. Christian ministry shares Jesus' kingdom message *through a community.*

The Catholic evangelist must always discern his or her direction in light of the believing community, for in union with this believing community the evangelist invites non-believers to share Jesus' message.

Parishes, Catholic schools, hospitals and orphanages can help Christians carry out their vocation by supporting people in their families and work, teaching clearly the message of Jesus and the church, celebrating Christian belief and practice in prayer and worship, serving the poor and oppressed, and witnessing to God's kingdom of justice, freedom, love and forgiveness.

Every act of a church organization does not necessarily further the cause of Catholic evangelization. Take the following example.

> Jim, married with several children, left a well-paying job in business to take a parish position. He knew the sacrifices this would entail, including salary and benefit cuts, plus evening meetings, but after prayer and reflection he decided to follow the Spirit's urgings and accept the position. Soon he got a feel for the work and was well accepted by parishioners and staff alike. His evaluations were very positive. He was doing a good job.
>
> Less than a year after beginning his job, Jim was told that his services were no longer required. The only reason — budget cutbacks. Jim was without a job less than a year after he left a well-paying job.
>
> Jim's situation is not unique in Catholic organizations. Sometimes employees are dismissed, with no reasons given except budget. In these cases, seniority, policies and positions do not seem to be significant factors.

Episodes like Jim's happen in parishes, diocesan offices, hospitals and Catholic schools. One parish administrator, in refusing to tell an employee why his contract was not renewed, said, "I do not have to give you any reasons. Our lawyer advised us to say nothing, for fear of lawsuits."

How can an evangelizing spirit develop in Catholic organizations that seem more interested in protecting themselves from lawsuits than in showing compassion and love? Decisions like the ones made in the above cases reveal the questionable state of policies, planning and budgeting in some Catholic organizations.

While legal matters and business concerns inevitably enter into the operations of Catholic institutions, charity and justice must always underlie the handling of these situations. When finances and legalism block justice and charity, one wonders how much evangelization can happen. One wonders further about the negative spin-off of such actions, when other people learn about this kind of treatment. Just because an institution is called "Catholic" one cannot automatically conclude that the spirit of the kingdom pervades it. If a church claims it is living out its call to evangelical ministry, its activities must be just and charitable.

Institutional sins must be named for what they are. There is no excuse for unjust treatment when good people become victims of inadequate management, political infighting and power plays. Even when budgetary constraints, poor job performance or personality conflicts require personnel changes, Christian ministry demands that tough decisions be carried out with openness, justice and charity. If church organizations fail to incorporate the kingdom message into their policies and actions, little authentic Christian ministry will occur.

The same applies to the individual Christian, for personal sin also blocks evangelization efforts. A Christian disciple evangelizes by acting charitably and justly, and by saying no to sin. By renouncing sin a Christian invites others to share faith in Jesus Christ and to accept the freedom, healing, hope and life promised by God's word.

Ministry and Evangelization

Two pitfalls exist when considering ministry and evangelization. The first pertains to institutional ministry; the second pertains to personal ministry.

Institutional Ministry

The shifting ministerial focus in Catholic dioceses and parishes brings with it a proliferation of ministries. With this comes organizational developments. Two consequences follow.

1. A lack of clear focus for ministry. Many dioceses and parishes are hard pressed to identify a common vision linking school ministry, religious education, liturgy, social action and other ministries. A diocesan staff member recently threw up her hands and said, "I don't know what we're all about. Diocesan offices are into their own thing. What is our common vision? To be effective, this diocese better get its act together." Her frustration came from the ambiguity she felt. Perhaps a renewed appreciation of evangelization, as the energizing center of all ministries directed to the kingdom of God, will give church ministries this needed focus.

2. Failure to link the various ministries adequately. When a clear focus for diocesan or parish ministry is lacking, various ministerial activities can become compartmentalized. This leads to "turf" building, competition and politics, as well as duplicated efforts. In parishes that lack a unified vision, youth ministry often has little to do with religious education or family ministry. Dioceses still struggle to relate school, religious education and liturgical ministries. Current parish and diocesan structures are often based more on business than on ministerial models centered on the kingdom of God. Evangelization has limited success where parish and diocesan models perpetuate the politics and competition that run counter to Jesus' message of love, cooperation and forgiveness.

Personal Ministry

The second pitfall lies in separating personal ministry or evangelization efforts from membership in the church.

Catholics generally do not identify their service to family, workplace or neighborhood as aspects of their Christian calling. They rarely consider family activities or their chosen work as opportunities for evangelization. In most cases, Catholics today fail to link their everyday lives with their active membership in the church.

Some Catholics, once active in church ministry, have another reaction. They have become disillusioned in working for the church, and their ministerial efforts have shifted to the world, with little reference to the Christian community. This is exemplified in the following episode.

A woman named Elsie often expressed angry feelings whenever church ministry was discussed. She refused to see how designated church ministers said anything to society.

For years, Elsie ministered in a parish and felt rebuffed. Finally, her hurt got the better of her. While still a believing Catholic, she prefers to exercise her ministry in the world.

This woman's unfortunate experience led her out of church ministry. In secular society, she feels more accepted in her ministerial efforts. Church leaders need to recognize hurting people like her, present in every parish, and to invite them to see how a truly evangelizing parish helps a Christian's ministry in the world.

Catholic evangelists and ministers are challenged to avoid the pitfall of disassociating individual evangelization efforts and ministry from the Christian community. While ministry is always based on one's baptismal calling, authentic Catholic ministry is always connected in some way to the Christian community. The Catholic approach holds communal and individual ministry in a delicate, creative tension. To deny individual ministry's link with community is as one-sided as to insist that all ministry must be designated in some way by the institutional church. Both reflect an incomplete understanding of church in the Catholic tradition.

A mature Christian acknowledges an individual call from God to proclaim the kingdom. This happens informally and formally. The first refers to human activities that reflect Jesus' teaching without directly mentioning his name. Loving parents, just business people and compassionate social workers evangelize informally. The second happens when teaching Jesus' message in catechesis, liturgy, sharing groups or personal witness. Parents, teachers, homilists and friends formally evangelize when speaking about God's message to those who do not know or believe.

To evangelize means to share faith. This faith sharing, also called "primary" or "core" evangelization, has several levels. Its most basic thrust is to non-believers, as the Christian community reaches out to "make disciples of all the nations" (Mt 28:19). Second, it is strongly oriented to unchurched, alienated, hurt or disinterested people who may or may not have faith. Often they believe in Jesus, but have problems with the church. Third, faith sharing is directed to children, youth or adults who are growing in faith. Evangelization deepens their belief in Jesus' message. Fourth, sharing faith is evangelization's constant call, inviting mature Christians to deeper levels of faith, dedication and insight. Evangelization affirms that Christians have something for which others desperately search, and invites these searchers to come and see.

This multi-faceted faith sharing, which core evangelization proclaims, is illustrated in the following diagram.

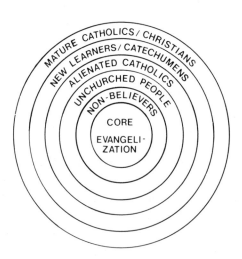

On each level, evangelization proclaims Jesus' teaching, as this is understood and practiced by the believing Catholic community.

Evangelizing Ministries

Evangelizing activity is the heart of all church ministry. To develop mature followers of Christ, willing to share their faith, is the goal of all church ministries and organizational structures. As we saw more fully in Chapter Five, the ministries of word, worship and service are the church's central evangelizing ministries.

The *ministry of the word* includes a parent teaching her child about God, a Catholic school religion class, parish catechetical sessions, adult religious enrichment, preaching, various scriptural and religious renewal programs, theology and more. Each helps people understand God's word and apply it to their lives. The heart of these endeavors includes communicating the lived reality of the paschal mystery and encouraging Christians to share their faith with others.

In the *ministry of worship* an individual or community celebrates the living Lord as central to life. Church liturgy provides opportunities to celebrate human joys and struggles as people link their experiences with Jesus' story. Baptism celebrates the beginnings of Christian life, marriage celebrates life shared together in a family, anointing of the sick celebrates the healing Lord present today and Eucharist celebrates the reality of Christ's presence, renewing people in community, word and sacrament.

Sacramental activities are special times when the community gathers to celebrate oneness in faith and to welcome others. Few better times exist to show warmth and welcome than on liturgical occasions such as Christmas, Easter, funerals, baptisms and weddings. Kind words and warm hearts at these times strengthen weak faith, nourish belief, reconcile alienated members and invite non-believers to follow Jesus. Liturgy should be a more powerful evangelizing activity than fish fries, bingos, festivals or parish picnics, because vibrant liturgies help people appreciate that Christian faith makes a difference.

Service activities include reaching out to the poor, helping the elderly and consoling the sick, which are part and parcel of Christian evangelization. When Christians show love and service, they inspire others to follow Jesus.

If a Christian reaches out in kindness, those served may ask, "What makes you tick?" "Why are you doing this for me?" or "What is your motivation?" The Christian evangelizer answers such questions by sharing the way the Christian faith motivates actions on behalf of charity and justice. Christians need not be afraid to speak about God. Such conversations help people appreciate Christ's message and the church's ministry.

To link church ministries with Jesus' call to evangelize, Christian activities must encourage people to follow the commandments, grow in deeper union with Christ and his body, love their neighbors more completely, practice the corporal works of mercy, reach out to those without faith, and welcome alienated Catholics and non-believers into the Christian community.

Evangelization, Ministry and Scripture

Ministry takes many forms, including a parent teaching a child about God and a parish reaching out to the poor. Ministry happens in formal and informal settings, as Christians share Jesus' message and their love. Where, though, do Catholics learn the good news of what they must do to be saved? The answer to this question has shifted focus in the Catholic community.

Before Vatican II, the Catholic answer was "by following the teachings and practices of the church." The church interpreted God's message for Catholics in almost every area of their lives. When I was a boy, my mom told me that as she was growing up, Catholics were forbidden to read the Bible. She remembered a priest telling her class that Protestants read the Bible, while Catholics followed the church's teaching. During my theological studies, the scriptures often were used to justify church teaching. I never perceived the scriptures as much more than a literal rendition of God's revelation.

After Vatican II, this changed and the church began to emphasize scripture. One of the most important tasks of church ministry is to stress the significance of scripture, for no real evangelization can happen without appreciation of the biblical message. These writings contain the earliest Christian witness to Jesus' life, teaching and ministry. A post-Vatican II answer to the question "Where do Catholics learn the good news of what they must do to be saved?" can be answered, "In the scriptures, which contain God's word, under the guidance and teaching of church leaders." Evangelization must always return to the scriptures to appreciate and deepen its proclamation of the good news.

The church exists to evangelize, and authentic church witness always evangelizes. Evangelizing ministry is the only legitimate way to be church.

EIGHT

Evangelization and Fundamentalism

Recently I spoke at the Los Angeles Religious Education Congress on "Fundamentalism and Catholic Evangelization." Afterward, more than 50 people stayed around for an hour asking how to help family members who joined fundamentalist churches. Inevitably, their stories about teenage children were similar. Several parents cried while saying, "What can we do? Our parish has little or nothing for young people. They are forbidden to use the gym and are chased off parish grounds. The fundamentalist church down the street welcomes them, offers scripture studies and provides hospitality. The youth are leaving our parish in droves and joining this church."

Parishes must listen to the cries of youth and involve them in parish life, including liturgy, ministerial services, parish councils and other church activities. Youth also need opportunities to pray together, study scripture, discuss problems related to drugs and dating, and develop community. Peer pressure during adolescence is strong. When parishes make youth feel welcome, this goes a long way to provide a Catholic environment where young people are at home.

Not only youth but large numbers of discontented Catholics of all ages are moving to fundamentalist churches. The following stories give some of the reasons behind this movement.

I took my car into a service station for an oil change. After I paid the bill, a young woman asked me, "Aren't you Father Hater?" "Yes," I answered. She replied, "Do you remember me? I'm Pam Jones."

I immediately recalled her as a sincere, interested high school student I had once taught. After a brief exchange, Pam hesitated and then said, "I am Catholic no longer, for I discovered the one true church of Jesus Christ." Then she named the fundamentalist congregation.

Pam was a very loyal Catholic youth, always ready to volunteer as a church festival worker or service minister. She attended Mass each Sunday and participated in other church activities including adult prayer groups.

But she told me, "I searched for community in the Catholic church, but never felt welcome. I wondered if people appreciated my efforts. With few activities for young people, I joined adult groups, but was out of place. I learned little about the Bible. Now my new church community supports and welcomes me, while I learn Jesus' teachings and the message of his church."

Pam's story is not unique. Another person I encountered found in fundamentalism what he had missed in the Catholic church.

While on a plane to New York, I sat beside a well-educated businessman in his early 30s. He noticed me reading a book on religion and asked about my faith. Soon he pulled out a bible, saying it was his "way of life." He continued, "I attended Catholic schools and went to Mass on Sundays until I was 20, but never felt part of Catholicism. Then a work associate invited me to the Christian church I presently attend. I now feel at home. Not until I joined this congregation did I appreciate the Bible as God's word. I live by it and carry a bible wherever I travel. It gives me wisdom, comfort and support."

The following story gives yet another example of people finding fundamentalist churches meeting their needs in ways the Catholic church has not.

José came from Mexico, where he was an active parish minister. He settled in a small Southwestern town. José attended Mass for several months, but felt unwelcome and almost unwanted. He spoke to the pastor and another parish minister after Sunday Mass and volunteered his services at the liturgy or other functions. "We'll let you know," they replied, but no one ever called him.

One day, several members of a small fundamentalist church visited José's trailer and invited him to attend a prayer weekend in their church. He went. Later they invited him to a training session in a nearby city. When José completed this, he was ordained a fundamentalist preacher.

He returned home and opened a store-front church next to his trailer. Other poor Hispanic people began knocking on José's door, sitting in his kitchen, studying scripture and talking about God. They said, "José, we want to join your church." "No," he replied, "you are Catholics. Go to the Catholic church on the hill."

They followed his advice and attended Mass, but felt isolated. They knocked on the rectory door. When no one answered they saw the sign, "Office Hours 10–4. Other times by appointment. In case of emergency call this number _____." These people called and got a recording, "Sorry, no one is here to receive your call. If you leave your name and number, we will call when we return." They left their names and numbers, but no one ever called them.

The people returned to José. After they came a second time, he accepted them into his church.

The above stories do not imply that Catholic parish renewal is not happening in many places. Through efforts like RENEW and CHRIST RENEWS HIS PARISH, many parishes have become welcoming ministerial communities, rooted in a personal involvement in scripture. Still, people's needs often are not met, evidenced by the large number of Catholics who join fundamentalist churches. This phenomenon invites all parishes, regardless of their place on the renewal spectrum, to look at parish ministry in light of the challenge of fundamentalism.

This chapter looks at the challenge of fundamentalism to evangelization. It should be noted that while this chapter does not offer a critique of fundamentalism, the church has serious problems with its doctrines and practices, rejecting many of them as inconsistent with Catholic teaching.

What is the appeal of Christian biblical fundamentalism? Part of the answer may lie in the fact that many roots that nourished pre-Vatican II Catholics have been removed and not replaced. Young Catholics, often unaware of the "basics" that their parents and grandparents learned, search for a firm anchor in an uncertain world. If their needs are not met in a Catholic parish, they may look elsewhere or drop out.

While Catholic parishes in the years after Vatican II may have neglected some basic elements, in no way should parishes move backward and try to return to an earlier era. Parishes today need to reappropriate core elements of Catholicism in light of contemporary needs.

People today yearn for stability and search for meaning. Contemporary culture gives them no significant road map. Many youths find little security in their families, and less in their parishes. Adults struggle with family solidarity, job pressures, elderly parents, drugs, alcoholism, social demands, and political and economic uncertainties.

Catholics, often in the mainstream of United States culture, reflect America's changing family patterns, affluence and work pressures. Time is at a premium, and human values are often under stress. Depersonalizing pressures invade family life, from third graders pushed to excel in sports activities to families that must plan ahead to be together for evening meals. Parishes try to balance spiritual responsibilities with financial, organizational and personnel pressures.

Some Catholics, searching for stability and roots, may identify with the certitude projected by fundamentalists. Certain elements in pre-Vatican II Catholicism resembled some aspects of contemporary biblical fundamentalism. Other Catholics, feeling no strong commitment to contemporary Catholicism, may discover the stability and community they desire in fundamentalism. Both groups identify critical elements necessary for Catholic parishioners to consider.

First, we will consider four key areas where fundamentalism seems to appeal to people today: 1) simple message; 2) personal message; 3) certitude, conviction and zeal; 4) community and hospitality. Then we will suggest concrete ways parishes can meet the same needs in their congregations.

1. *Simple Message.* Fundamentalists teach a simple message, namely, "The Bible is God's word! Live by it and be saved!" In an increasingly complex world, their absolutely literal interpretation of the Bible appeals to many people, giving them absolute answers in uncertain times.

2. *Personal Message.* Fundamentalism emphasizes Jesus as a personal Lord and savior. This message addresses the human search for holiness, intimacy and belonging. A sick, broken individual may shy away from people. A feeling of a special bonding with Jesus can be powerful. It is easy to understand why many hurting, broken people sit by TV sets praying for healing or attend churches that stress Jesus as healer and Lord.

Also, a personal savior is appealing in contrast to the institutional complexity of many church organizations. Jesus' way cannot be as complex as parishes sometimes make it. Church bureaucracy and the over-professionalization of ministries may lead people to say, "Enough! I need spiritual nourishment, not another corporate organization."

3. *Certitude, Conviction and Zeal.* Fundamentalists preach and proselytize with certitude, conviction and zeal. Their enthusiasm, while offensive to some people, impresses others, who search for truths to hold onto and truths to believe.

4. *Community and Hospitality.* Fundamentalists emphasize community and hospitality. They welcome strangers and

make them feel important. Ministries of hospitality and welcoming are given high priority. In a mobile country, where the average person moves once every three years and makes a long distance move once every five years, offering welcome to the newcomer is an important ministry.

Implications for Catholic Parishes

One might ask, "What can parishes do to provide hospitality, community, roots, answers, stability and certitude for today's Catholics?" The following conclusions invite Catholic parishes to address these issues in concrete and helpful ways as a means of effective evangelization.

1. *Center parish ministry on Jesus' teaching about the kingdom of God.* Vatican II emphasized that the church exists to proclaim God's kingdom. This kingdom is present wherever God is present. Jesus stressed God's special presence with poor, hurting people, encouraging them to become whole. The goal of the kingdom is life and freedom, where broken people are healed and reconciled.

As I travel across the country giving lectures, teaching and counseling, I notice alarming numbers of people suffering through divorce, alcoholism, drugs, loneliness, meaninglessness, poverty, sickness, bereavement and old age. Parishes are challenged to offer such people healing and reconciliation through a conversion process that enables them to see and understand in a new way. Conversion is often accelerated during times of personal tragedy when support, especially family support, is important. Family support is reinforced by friends, parish staff members and ministry groups like Saint Vincent de Paul.

The kingdom message, discovered through support and encouragement, helps facilitate ongoing conversion. How parishes treat hurting people often influences their long-term commitment to Catholicism. The kingdom message is also proclaimed in homilies and catechesis. Information about faith or church teaching is only one aspect influencing personal conversion. More important is helping people see the kingdom's significance in their lives.

Homilies, catechesis and parish ministries should apply Christian belief to family and work. People look for help in dealing with practical concerns, especially those involving their children. Parishes that provide such opportunities reap many blessings. Family people look to parishes for guidance in their struggle to become holy families. Parish ministry can teach people to appreciate the challenges of their daily work as a vital aspect of their Christian vocation, when work is carried out in the spirit of Christ.

Parish ministry can also help people deal with the pressures of work. The marketplace generates tremendous pressures in the struggle to balance family and work responsibilities. Often families are torn apart because work-demands pull family members in different directions. A parish helps families balance commitments and work obligations by taking a serious look at how parish responsibilities take people away from their families.

Jesus' special presence with poor, hurting people challenges every parish to give top priority to the unemployed, to people trying to overcome drug and alcohol dependencies, to the broken and abandoned of whatever age, and to the lonely.

A parish that genuinely lives the kingdom message in all aspects of its ministry will be filled with life, hope and enthusiasm.

2. *Preach and teach a simple message.*   Jesus taught in parables and stories. He spoke ordinary language, using imagery people understood. His message touched the hurting, broken dimensions of their lives.

Homilists and catechists can learn an important lesson from Jesus. People are not motivated by sophisticated theology or biblical exegesis. They crave good, common-sense teaching. Consequently, priests might depend less on prepackaged homily helps and concentrate more on applying Sunday biblical readings to people's lives, by speaking about everyday experiences of children, youth, senior citizens, neighbors, nature, work, single people and families. Scripture comes alive when illustrated in flesh and blood stories that touch people's hearts.

The same applies to catechetical sessions. Catechesis in the RCIA often is successful because catechumens relate the biblical message to their lives. This link is the paradigm for all catechesis. Catechists need to be sensitive to the situations of those being catechized, and to encourage them to come to deeper insights about themselves in light of scripture and church teaching.

Fundamentalists remind Catholics of a central element in proclaiming God's word when they insist on "teaching something definite." Catechesis that does not center around essential Catholic teaching, rooted in strong scripture study, is inadequate and incomplete.

3. *Base all parish activities on Christian community and welcome.*   The gospels picture people flocking to Jesus. He must have made them feel welcome. Parishes must make people feel welcome at all church functions. This responsibility extends from ushers, greeters and liturgical ministers to housekeepers, secretaries and janitors. Parishes are challenged to develop a "welcoming spirit" that permeates the entire community, beginning in families and extending to church and neighborhood affairs.

In a frantic society filled with family problems, social conflicts and job pressures, people need a place to feel at home and welcome. The parish can provide an environment for all people — young or old, rich or poor — to gather, hear God's word, break bread and resolve to go out and live the Christian message. Welcome and hospitality are rooted in people's common brotherhood and sisterhood. Contemporary Catholic success stories in evangelization and renewal always stress welcome and hospitality.

Jesus' life inspired the first Christians to form community. Then, as now, community means two or more people sharing common traditions, values and practices on an ultimate level. Functional activities do not in themselves bring community but can provide occasions for people to share deep community bonds.

Ultimate experiences such as love, trust and sacrifice help people realize their equality before God.

Welcome happens on an ultimate, not functional, level. New parishioners want to hear more than "Welcome to the parish! Here are your envelopes." Senior citizens want to be important parish members. Parents preparing for a child's baptism need special attention. Lapsed Catholics planning for marriage or inquiring about their child's baptism must be handled pastorally and given every benefit of the doubt. Youth ministry needs to be developed.

Central to proclaiming a kingdom message is living it. A welcoming parish invites parishioners and visitors to call upon staff members and other parishioners in time of need. Freedom to ask for help usually happens when people representing the parish community first reach out to others. This can happen in the church, at the rectory, in the supermarket or during a home visit. People hesitate to seek help unless they know their requests will be heeded, for they are refused enough in society.

4. *Develop a parish spirit of pride, zeal, certitude and con-viction that carries over into the parishioner's family and work.* Catholics need a spiritual challenge. To be meaningful, faith must become a part of life, inspiring people to do good, warning them to refrain from evil, illuminating them to see the right way in an ambiguous world. Catholic identity must be re-established in the post-Vatican II church by implementing the deepest movements of the Spirit, which revolve around kingdom themes and a new appreciation of the entire community's responsiblity for ministry.

Today, biblical fundamentalists show certitude and zeal. But these attitudes are not new to Catholics; they were present before Vatican II. In working for a kingdom of peace and justice, these qualities will re-emerge, as Catholics ground their lives in faith and develop lay ministry.

Catholic pride begins in families. If parents frequently criti-cize parish, school, clergy and pastoral ministers, what does this say to their children? If parents are often away from their families at parish meetings or activities, what do children conclude about a parish that robs them of parental time? This does not mean that parents should avoid being honest about parish strengths and weaknesses. Children need to learn this lesson. Nor does it imply that parents should drop out of all church activities. It does mean, however, that positive, constructive attitudes are necessary to encourage family members to regard the parish as an important, useful aspect of their lives. It also means that prudence is necessary when family members decide how much time to spend in parish ministry and how much time to spend at home.

Positive attitudes encourage children, youth and adults. When this happens, zeal and enthusiasm carry over to friends, neighbors, work associates and parishes. Then it is easier to take pride in being Catholic.

5. *Re-emphasize the basics of the Catholic faith.* When Catholics know who they are and what they are about, pride and certitude follow. To help this happen, parishes can provide varied opportunities for scripture study, prayer and catechesis at all age levels. Catechesis is a top ministerial priority, for many Catholics today are "religiously illiterate," with little knowledge of scripture, prayer or basic Catholic teaching.

The time has come to focus on the basics of the Catholic faith. Catechetically, this means teaching the meaning of prayer, scripture, Mass, sacraments, morality, sin, Jesus, church and Catholic doctrine. Liturgically, it means appreciating the Mass, sacraments, liturgical year, family devotions and personal prayer. Many young Catholics have a foggy understanding of the Mass and little insight into prayer. After a class session on the Mass with an upper-level, undergraduate theology class, some students reacted in anger. This anger surfaced when they realized that they never before learned the Eucharist's meaning and significance, in spite of many years of Catholic education.

One 21-year-old religious studies major said, "I am a liturgical minister and received Catholic education since I was 6 years old. Why was I not taught this before? For the first time I appreciate why the Mass is important for Catholics." In this class students found the discussions on prayer fascinating. Few had previously studied prayer. Their curiosity reminded me of the scripture passage where Jesus' disciples asked him, "Lord, teach us to pray..." (Lk 11:1). People today also need guidance and direction. This same class showed ignorance, yet interest, when discussing sin and conscience formation. In a world where sin and guilt are real, people need the church's help to deal with these realities.

6. *Encourage lay leadership.*   Enthusiasm and conviction follow when Catholic lay people accept responsibility for their parishes. The decline in the numbers of priests and sisters has a positive side. If this had never happened, it would have been difficult for lay people to move into church leadership positions. Parish stability rests in the community, not merely in the pastor. Pastors move on, communities remain. Consequently, pastoral leadership and parish appointments must include community participation and responsibility. If this happens, "Catholic spirit" will re-emerge with new confidence.

7. *Develop a love for and knowledge of the scriptures.*   Perhaps the most important challenge fundamentalism offers Catholics is to know and love the scriptures. The Christian scriptures are "Catholic writings"; it's about time Catholics accept them as such. Daily scripture reading can help fill up the spiritual vacuum many Catholics feel.

Catholic parishes perform a tremendous service when they base their ministerial efforts on love for and appreciation of the scriptures. It is sad to hear a former Catholic say, "I left the Catholic church and joined a Protestant community to learn about Jesus' teachings in the scriptures."

How Catholic parishes address this challenge may vary from place to place, but can include the following:

— a love for and knowledge of the scriptures on the part of the pastor and ministerial team;

— opportunities for parishioners to study the scriptures both in the parish setting and in people's homes;

— practical ways for people to learn more about the scriptures and how to pray with them;

— regular parish opportunities for people to pray with scripture;

— a parish resource center, where bibles, practical commentaries, books and tapes about the scriptures can be borrowed or purchased;

— a commitment to begin each parish project, meeting or session by listening to God's biblical word;

— opportunities for children and youth to learn about scripture;

— opportunities for parents to learn how to teach scripture to their children;

— retreats and days of renewal based on scripture;

— catechetical sessions for children, youth and adults, including catechesis in Catholic schools, which stress the centrality of the scriptures, especially the Christian scriptures;

— a parish style that relates all social and service functions in some way to the scriptures (for example, before a St. Vincent de Paul or similar meeting, a participant can read a passage from scripture and discuss or pray about how the ministerial activities that the group is about to consider relate to Jesus' words and deeds);

— homilies centered on helping people to apply the scriptures to their everyday lives.

Parishes are challenged to re-examine their spirit, style and organizational structures to see whether they give people's needs sufficient consideration. This may require reviewing a parish's philosophy and planning process, and giving top priority to people's needs, solid teaching, good liturgies and service activities. A consolidated effort is necessary to accomplish this goal — getting out into the neighborhood, expressing concern for the poor and compassion for sick, hurting and alienated people, asking for parishioners' opinions, listening to them, making parish functions opportunities for welcome, and dedicating the parish to ongoing spiritual renewal based on gospel values.

Catholic parishes are challenged not to *do* more, but to *be* more — to be more welcoming, reconciling, healing and available as they strive to help parishioners become aware of basic Catholic beliefs and practices.

NINE

Evangelization
and Spirituality

Spirituality is the quest for God. It never happens in a vacuum. It is deeply influenced by family and culture, for God shares divine life through other people, who influence our yes of faith. Spirituality is rooted in shared faith. This chapter considers spirituality and evangelization in four sections: the challenges of contemporary culture, the process of spirituality, elements required for an evangelistic spirituality and the consequences of spirituality and evangelization for parish and family.

The Challenge of Contemporary Culture

Evangelization happens within the context of culture. Contemporary United States culture rests on technology. Technology is a great gift. Used properly, it can build the earth, and bring peace, justice and freedom. It offers untold possibilities for good when people root their lives in ultimate values (love, justice and truth) and see technology and possessions as means to an end, not as ends in themselves.

Modern technology shapes values and priorities. It affords wonderful opportunities for building a better world through unlimited possibilities for communication, research and travel. But there is a flip side to these benefits. Television often stresses superficiality, relativism, possessions, money, sex and power; the "anti-hero" becomes a god. Computers canonize a quantified, functional worldview that knows no variations and leaves little room for ultimate values.

Cultural values, ritualized in the media, affect family life. Many people resemble a television set — turn on in the morning, go-go-go all day, take an occasional time out for a commercial, eat, shop, love on the run and turn off to sleep after the 11 o'clock news.

People who live like this do not have the "sacred" time or space in which to unwind, enjoy nature, experience intimacy, pray or keep Sunday as the Lord's day. Sunday exists to catch up on the week's chores. Quantifiable, functional values have priority and there is little depth to life. Sheer survival becomes the ultimate goal.

Families struggle to survive with little help from society, church and family traditions that once formed a solid set of values. They tread uncharted paths, influenced by television, movies, music, books and advertising.

Many families try hard to share ultimate values, intimacy and love, but secular pressures are great. It is easy to fall into the trap of functionalism without realizing it. A Catholic school teacher who had been teaching second grade for more than 30 years said, "I have never taught children before who were so spiritually deprived. Often, they experience the worst kind of spiritual deprivation. Many parents seldom pray with their children or speak about God. Except for school time, children are often in day care from 6:30 a.m. to 6:30 p.m. After this, they are shuffled to fast-food restaurants and through shopping centers well into the evening. They get so many things to appease them that Christmas and Easter have little value."

Marital stress, especially divorce, can devastate children. One third-grade boy recently said, "My daddy's latest girlfriend likes our hamster more than me."

A sixth-grade religion teacher said, "By this age, many kids build a wall around themselves. They have to be 'cool.' To show emotion means running the risk of getting hurt." Many children have also assimilated a value system in which success and status are more important than integrity. The same sixth-grade teacher said, "One girl, after hearing Jesus' story, replied, 'Did you say that Jesus was a carpenter? How do you expect us to follow him, if he was only a carpenter?'"

Children need more time spent in relaxed, loving relationships with their parents. The negative scenarios above do not deny that many loving families struggle successfully to maintain healthy, positive relationships. But today's crisis in family life challenges Christians to look seriously at their own relationships and values.

The Christian community can make a tremendous contribution by challenging society to live by deep and authentic values while drawing on the rich potential of modern technology. Jesus' teachings offer a powerful message for people desperately trying to make sense out of their fast-paced lives.

Spirituality: A Process

Evangelization means simply "sharing the good news of God's love and forgiveness." This begins in the family. Spirituality is the ongoing result of a response to evangelization. Like evangelization, spirituality is a process rooted in creation, filtered through community and influenced by institutions. Six elements have significance for spirituality and evangelization.

1. *Culture has a powerful influence on spiritual formation.* I grew up in a Catholic family and neighborhood, attended Catholic schools and took an active part in parish functions. During these years spirituality meshed with church, neighborhood and family. Church rituals and personal prayer were consistent in life.

After high school, I entered the college seminary and left family, friends and a comfortable spirituality to enter a new world where spirituality became a regimentation of formal prayer, with little spontaneity and freedom. One day I asked myself, "Where is the God I felt so close to as a youth?"

This simple example from my own story illustrates what a powerful influence institutions such as family and church can have in forming spirituality.

2. *Efforts to facilitate spiritual growth in family, school or parish must be sensitive to a person's individual spiritual tendencies.*   This requires great flexibility. Where sensitivity to individual or cultural needs is absent, negative results usually follow. For example, Maria, a Hispanic woman, entered a convent but lasted only one year. Her spiritual traditions were not respected; she had to comply with white, middle class, European values. Black men who entered the seminary often had a similarly negative experience.

3. *Regardless of cultural pressures, humans are carried along by a force greater than themselves.*   Absolute trust in this "greater force" (God) directing human life is essential for spiritual growth. Each person must be true to God's invitation that says, "Come, follow me." Who can say why some people have this or that gift? This or that opportunity? Why some people suffer so much? The bottom line is what a person learns from such experiences, not the experiences themselves.

4. *Christian spirituality is rooted in personal gifts and the baptismal calling.*   When people forget their roots and take refuge behind roles or masks, their lives lose focus. To be a loving spouse or mother, Sally must first be Sally, who is also a mother and spouse. Jim, to be true to himself, first must be Jim, who is also a businessman, rather than a businessman named Jim. Recognizing individual talents enables people to see that Christian spirituality calls them to be faithful to the way their personal gifts, rooted in the Spirit, direct them to the kingdom of God.

5. *God works in people's hearts, even in situations involving pain and suffering.*   God is present in dysfunctional families and seemingly lifeless parishes. Reflecting on this aspect of the spiritual journey gives one hope when dealing with struggling

people or experiencing boring liturgies or poor catechesis. God is always present, especially with poor, hurting people.

6. *The deepest motivating force pulling mature Christians into the future is belief in God's presence and life's meaning.* Faith roots Christian spirituality; by saying yes to the Spirit within, people further God's creative designs.

Evangelization and Spirituality

These six elements set the stage for a deeper consideration of evangelization and spirituality. Pre-Vatican II spirituality stressed following God's will by following church beliefs and practices. Post-Vatican II spirituality focuses on responding to God by giving attention to God's kingdom. These two types of spirituality are not mutually exclusive; their ultimate goal of union with God is the same, but the approaches differ.

Contemporary spirituality is linked with evangelization. This means spirituality:

— focuses on the kingdom;

— needs the Christian community to support this kingdom focus;

— acknowledges God's presence in family, marketplace and society;

— accepts the responsibility to continue God's creative activity in the world;

— responds to Jesus' call to challenge unjust social and church structures;

— bases its orientation on baptism and the common priesthood of all Christians;

— recognizes the need for sacred time to pray and reflect;

— develops a bonding with the Christian community, especially its liturgical and sacramental life;

— continues to probe God's presence in life through relating God's word in scripture to human experience;

— places high regard on spiritual reading and church
teaching as solid grounding for individual and communal spirituality.

These characteristics of evangelistic spirituality challenge individuals and parishes to consider how the Christian community
helps people search for meaning and purpose in lives that often
have little unity. The heart of this quest involves listening and
responding to the Spirit of God.

Holistic Spirituality

Shortly after my ordination, Mom attended a Mass where I
was the celebrant. Afterward, in discussing my homily, she said,
"Bob, tell stories." Her words helped me link the scriptures more
deeply with life. When I began to tell stories, my preaching
changed. "Why does everyone listen," I wondered, "when a
story is told? Why do they get distracted with more technical
explanations?" Soon I realized that a story appeals to the whole
person — emotions, spirit and mind — while explanations or
examples appeal primarily to the mind.

Evangelistic spirituality, centered on discovering God through
shared faith, begins in the human story. Effective spirituality
touches people's stories. Examples include spiritual companion-
ing, shared faith experiences, directed retreats, preached retreats
inviting a person to see God working in life and more. Parish
spirituality is inadequate if it fails to help people sort out the
Spirit's role in work, family and social life. A spirituality that
centers on the story provides a focal point enabling people to develop a value system from within, rather than having one imposed
from without.

I learned something about the importance of story from the
Native Americans. For them, "the story" frames life — creation
stories, hero myths and other tribal stories set the parameters
for existence. These stories, explaining holistically why things
are as they are, make more sense to the fullness of a person's
experience than rational analysis. Community and individual
stories help people make sense of life. For example, Grandma

Harie's faith (the Christian story) gives her great reverence for the Eucharist. Mark's faith (the Christian story) inspires him to work with prisoners. Billy's parents' divorce and struggle with alcoholism (his family story) brings him fear when he wonders whether he should marry. Story is essential to life, for story reveals who we are, and why we are as we are.

Story is also where God is present. To discover God's presence in the human heart, look to the story. Spirituality based on a person's story invites one to search for maturity.

Becoming mature is a lifelong process. Some 14 year olds are mature for their age, while some 40 year olds are immature. Maturity is seen in the context of one's story. Respecting the uniqueness of every person means acknowledging the personal and social factors operative in personal growth.

As people reach out to life, they encounter blocks and obstacles. For example, Sam was physically abused as a child. He became quiet and timid, afraid of more rejection. This surfaced dramatically in adolescence, when he refused to go to high school. Therapy traced his fear to early abuse. Sam needs to overcome this block before he can develop his potential. In another case, Bill and Mary, married for 17 years, got a divorce after Bill began dating another woman. Mary, devastated by the extramarital affair, became sullen and depressed. It took five years before she got on with her life.

In both examples, traumatic events blocked the person's journey to maturity. Lesser examples include failing an examination, being insulted at a party or having a fight at home. These situations need to be faced before one can adequately reach out. Some blocks may be handled in a few days, others take years.

To become mature every person must reach out to life. Small babies move their hands and arms. Toddlers explore their surroundings. Adolescents begin a search for meaning in their lives. Adults move into a wide variety of experiences that connect them with their inner selves and with other people. This reaching out is essential if a person is to probe life's mysteries and to appreciate God's presence. When a person reaches out, life always responds positively or negatively. As this occurs, a person learns.

When I was a boy, my family supported, affirmed and loved me. I remember Dad playing ball with me, our family going on vacations, and Mom helping me with my homework. Grade and high school continued this supportive environment. I developed self-confidence and a positive outlook in the ups and downs of growing toward maturity through childhood and adolescence. During this growth stage, self-reflection helped me understand who I was. This self-reflection was rooted in my acceptance by family, school and neighbors. I sorted this out to the degree that a child and adolescent could do so. Rejection by a few classmates during these years was seen in the broader context of a loving environment.

When I first went to the seminary, the positive environment changed. The seminary's rigor, impersonality and competition contrasted sharply with my home.

One day, while I was discussing some matter at an assembly, I was ridiculed by a professor. He shredded me with sarcasm. My confidence was shattered. This event made me insecure when speaking publicly. For twelve years after this event, in public speeches, I fell into a falsetto tone. Finally, four years after ordination, when I moved into a very supportive environment, I returned to my natural speaking ways.

What happens — success, affirmation, disappointment, failure — influences one's self-image. This happens on a subconscious level. Self-reflection, or taking the time to ask questions about who we are and how events affect us, can help us grow toward maturity as we deal with these influences. The ever-present God, assisted by family, friends and counselors, moves us to new levels of awareness.

Through self-reflection, an individual gradually comes to clearer personal insight. This recognition is basic for a mature life. Personal goals ground the way an individual reaches out to life. Self-reflection helps a person ascertain which ones are realistic. Everyone has gifts and limits. Until a person appreciates the implications of this reality, he or she will search for impossible dreams or shy away from realistic opportunities.

Personal outreach needs a focus. Gradually, through life's give and take, a person sets directions for his or her life. We gravitate toward certain people and avoid others. We pursue particular career objectives and develop life patterns. We form a value system, influenced by the give and take of our experiences.

Secular society perpetrates a massive fraud when it tells people that functional values bring happiness. Unless a person roots life in ultimate values, deep human maturity is not possible.

A mature person's value system is consistently directive; ultimate values help people decide when to say yes and when to say no. Two stories illustrate this point:

> Michael accepted a promotion as vice president of a large corporation. Soon management directed him to perform actions not consistent with his values. His high salary tempted him to go along with their orders. His value system, honed and refined through his family, faith and prayer, told him otherwise. Michael quit his job, after consultation with his wife and four children. They asked for God's help and decided that each family member would work to support the family, rather than compromise Michael's values.

> Sally, a college sophomore, attended a party with friends. Many students, including her date, began to smoke marijuana. One man made sexual advances to her. Insulted and under pressure, she left.

Michael's and Sally's decisions reflect a quality of a mature person, namely, a consistent value system that they refused to compromise.

Evangelistic Spirituality

Evangelistic spirituality, resting on creation and the kingdom of God, takes various shapes and directions, depending on the time, culture, environment, group and individual. This section considers requirements for, and characteristics of, evangelistic spirituality.

Requirements for Evangelistic Spirituality

People today crave direction, certitude and roots. The Catholic faith can offer people a direction and focus. Catholic beliefs and practices are rooted in Jesus' teaching on the kingdom of God. While the Catholic faith acknowledges personal freedom, it invites people to share a way of life.

Evangelization centers around sharing faith, which gives direction to people's lives. Evangelistic spirituality requires:

— knowing Jesus' teaching on creation and the kingdom;

— appreciating Catholic beliefs and practices;

— making Jesus' way and church life important aspects of one's life and work;

— acknowledging family and work as central places to share faith;

— developing a spirituality that integrates personal life, family, work, society and church into a holistic perspective;

— providing Christian witness;

— inviting others, through deeds and words, to follow Jesus;

— welcoming interested persons to investigate the Catholic faith;

— acknowledging God's presence in creation, culture, various Christian denominations, the Jewish faith and world religions.

— allowing Christian values to be unifying factors in personal and communal life.

Evangelistic spirituality invites people to reach out to others. This may include sharing faith in a family, struggling for justice in society or participating in missionary activities.

Evangelistic spirituality also acknowledges that spirituality, rooted in faith, influences actions. A mature religious person's life revolves around faith, which challenges society's materialistic orientation and invites people to focus on love, justice, mercy and compassion.

Evangelistic spirituality continually invites people to respond to God's revelations. Spirituality may be evident in people with little or no church affiliation. God's mysterious working at times leads people with little or no family faith to deep personal belief and action. Their God-given gifts often encourage them to develop ultimate values and move them toward social awareness or humanitarian concerns. Dialogue with such good people teaches Christians about Jesus' call to serve the poor and needy.

Individually and collectively, more and more people are searching for ways to know themselves. Self-help books, support groups, counseling, spiritual direction and other techniques continue to grow in popularity. Evangelistic spirituality offers a valuable opportunity in this regard. It says, "All authentic reflection is based on a relationship with God." Christians believe God is loving, healing, holy, just, powerful and beyond human comprehension. Christians also believe that human beings, created in God's image, are called to become holy and to live forever with God.

Evangelistic spirituality invites Christians to learn more about God by reflecting on their experiences, Jesus' teaching and the church's beliefs and practices. These are illustrated in the following stories:

> Esther and Bill, both unmarried, lived together. Until they attended a parish renewal session, neither thought much about the implications of their way of life in light of Jesus' teaching, Christian belief and the negative example this lifestyle gave to family members and neighbors. This new realization moved them to live apart until they made a decision about marriage.

> Irma, a bookkeeper in a business office, altered the books regularly at the request of her boss. Not until she heard a homily about justice did Irma seriously connect Jesus' teaching on justice with her responsibility to live justly.

The self-reflection associated with evangelistic spirituality invites

Catholics to join the various segments of their lives (work, family, religion) into a unified whole.

Characteristics of Evangelistic Spirituality

Evangelistic spirituality sees Jesus as a fully human and fully mature individual. The following characteristics root a mature evangelistic spirituality in this view of Jesus' life and in solid psychological insights.

— *Evangelistic spirituality situates the person's relationship with God and the world in creation.*

— *Jesus' spirituality links humans with God in his teaching on the kingdom, found in the Christian scriptures.* A kingdom-based spirituality sees healing, forgiveness and reconciliation as center points linking broken humanity with God. Becoming fully human means loving God, serving others and working for justice.

— *Evangelistic spirituality sees becoming a full, holy person as a lifelong quest.* The prologue of John's gospel describes the Word (Jesus) as existing from the beginning and disclosing himself in time. This hints at a transcendent quest, inviting every person to join with Jesus in a lifelong journey to discover God.

— *A spirituality based on sharing faith is alive with God's Spirit.* It motivates one to action by stressing the human vocation to share God's life with others. A spirituality based in faith brings life and freedom into the active search for meaning.

— *Evangelistic spirituality includes all aspects of human life, especially family, personal life, work, friends, society, parish and nature.* It treats people of other races and religions as God's children, acknowledges different methods of prayer and spirituality and allows for diversity. The spiritually mature person acknowledges the whole world as the arena of God's presence.

— *Evangelistic spirituality distinguishes good from evil, virtue from sin, and stresses a steady course and coherent value system in a person's life journey.* A consistently directive motivation provides a unifying basis upon which to decide and act, whether in church, at home, with friends or in the marketplace.

— *A spiritually mature person is open to change and growth, eager to investigate life and to probe deeply the meaning of faith.* This person overcomes fear with faith and guilt with love, and is open to learning from various religious and secular sources.

— *Spiritual maturity recognizes that all people are equal before God.* This leads to dialogue where people are respected, not controlled or manipulated. Evangelistic spirituality acknowledges that God's love often comes through human love. A spiritually mature person knows the importance of love, which begins in God.

— *Evangelistic spirituality brings new insights, for it discerns human activities in light of God's revelation, church teaching and social response.* A spiritually mature person acknowledges the Holy Spirit as the ultimate source of human wisdom and insight.

— *The spiritually mature person recognizes people's limits and sees the humor in an all-wise God becoming human and dying for sinful creatures.* This paradox is the basis for Christian faith. Evangelistic spirituality acknowledges God's playfulness, patience with weak human beings and tolerance of failure, as well as God's justice, fairness and truth. The spiritually mature person, while admitting guilt and fear, is not overcome by them. This humorous and playful characteristic of evangelistic spirituality reminds the spiritually mature person that humans are human and God is God.

If God loves people, they must love one another; if God forgives humans, they must forgive themselves and others. Evangelistic spirituality admits human limits, faults, sins and the folly of taking oneself too seriously. It is not complacent or excusing, but it accepts life after death, hope in difficult times and new opportunities after failures.

Evangelization finds its deepest meaning in the spiritual quest, where God's presence in creation reaches fulfillment. Church ministry will be effective to the degree that it responds to the spiritual yearnings present in people's hearts and to the quest often already begun in their lives.

Consequences for Parishes and Families

Recently a parent said, "Why doesn't the parish do more to support families? We get little help from society and not much more from the church. Parishes need to make a commitment to help families spiritually. Unless they do, parishes will become increasingly irrelevant."

How can parishes address her challenge? Parish evangelization must begin by taking into account the way that culture influences families. To succeed, evangelization must be rooted in the family. How this happens will vary from parish to parish. Some practical questions may help:

—   To what extent is a family focus central to all parish activities? Do parish events (RCIA, catechetics, school functions, children's sporting activities and other parish events) separate or bring together members of the same family?

—   How is family life affected when a parishioner spends a great deal of time in parish ministry (hanging around the church)? Does the parish send out a subtle message about values by pulling busy people away from their homes to work around the church?

—   Do Sunday homilies support families and give practical ways to apply scripture readings to everyday life?

— Do parish priorities give high value to supporting hurting families, to acknowledging single parent/divorced/blended families, and to stressing that single people are important family and church members?

— How do parish ministers and programs teach parishioners, especially children and youth, the skills necessary to develop Christian values in a computerized, technological culture?

The responsibility for alleviating today's spiritual hunger does not lie solely with the parish, however. Family members must also reflect on their own priorities. The following questions may provide some guidance:

Leveling of values — When values center on money and possessions, little depth and intimacy exist. What are your values? Which ones are out of focus?

Priorities — To live a Christian life in today's world, one must establish priorities. How are your priorities reflected in lifestyle and time commitment? What about intimacy and the need for quality time with family members? What can be done to re-establish your priorities?

Living skills — Skills for everyday living are most deeply taught in the family. What skills for living are being taught in your family? Are they ultimate — love, forgiveness, justice — or functional — money, greed, jealousy, cutting corners?

Controlling mass media — People control TV or it controls them. Do you control what your children watch on TV? What about what you watch? Does TV inhibit the communication between family members? How do you help your children develop the skills necessary to sift out acceptable and unacceptable moral values in TV programming and advertising?

Keep Sunday holy — Sunday is God's day, set aside for God's honor and our personal renewal. Remember that skipping Sunday Mass sends negative signals to children. Is Sunday much of a holy day in your family? What more can you do to make Sunday a family day? You might ask your parish to cut out all meetings on Sunday and limit activities to Mass, religious instruction and relaxation.

Pray — Family prayer acknowledges God's presence in the home and solidifies family relationships. What are the best ways and times for your family to pray together? What kind of example do you as parents show to children by praying with them and each other?

Intimacy — People are born in love and grow through love. Do you have communication problems with certain family members? How can this improve? What is your level of intimacy with each family member? How can you grow together in love?

If people experience God's love in the love they have for one another and share this love in word and deed, spirituality and evangelization will take care of themselves. The Christian message is taught, celebrated and lived when Jesus' way becomes our way. In the depths of human love the deepest manifestation of God's good news is revealed.

TEN

Evangelization and Pastoral Life: A Practical Process

Parishes search for ways to evangelize more effectively. This chapter gives practical suggestions for parish evangelization. The chapter is divided into three sections: evangelization's goal of proclaiming God's good news of salvation, the importance of knowing people's needs and responding to them, and practical ways for a parish to proceed.

Proclaiming God's Good News of Salvation

Evangelization begins by acknowledging God's presence in life. Creation's mystery hints at God's love, beauty and compassion. At the same time, creation depicts struggle, sorrow and death. All great religious traditions try to reconcile the ambiguities surrounding a wonderful, yet broken world.

Christian evangelization faces human paradoxes in light of Jesus' life and teachings. A Christian evangelist's first responsibility is to know Jesus' message. This demands that parish evangelization emphasizes the scriptures as God's word. All other aspects of Christian evangelization rest upon God's revealed word. Once God's word is appreciated, people become enthusiastic about sharing it.

Catholic evangelization interprets God's word in light of Catholic traditions. Since the Christian scriptures flowed from community beliefs, Catholic tradition plays a guiding and overseeing role, insuring that God's word is maintained and interpreted as Jesus proclaimed it.

The most basic principle of Catholic evangelization is: "Stress the scriptures and help people understand Jesus' message, so they can apply it to their lives and share it with others." This begins in the family and is fostered in the parish. If this principle is not given a high priority, parish renewal can have only limited success. People need to know God's word if Catholic evangelization is to bear fruit.

Knowing People's Needs and Responding to Them

A parish team asked me to consult with them about their youth religious education program. The team included seven well-prepared catechists sincerely interested in youth work. They developed their program and advertised it. The syllabus, teachers and support staff were in place. The first evening, with seven teachers prepared to teach, no young people came.

As we discussed their problem, it became clear that neither the program nor the time fit the students' needs. Every week over 60 teenagers, who attended seven different public schools, came to the parish to play volleyball and basketball on the evening *before* the scheduled religion classes.

After meetings between youth ministers and catechists it was decided to merge catechesis, socials and sports into one total youth ministry program.

The original organizers of the religion program did not recognize the students' needs and did not consult them. When this happens, parish efforts often fail.

The above episode is often repeated in parish ministry. Parish evangelization has limited results if people's needs are not known or met. The first requirement for successful parish evangelization is to ascertain people's needs. This is illustrated in the following story.

When the population of a parish in the southwestern United States shifted to predominantly poor Mexican-Americans, it continued to operate with a White-Anglo mentality. The pastor and parish ministers were rarely seen in the neighborhood. But fundamentalist preachers and parishioners knocked on doors, inviting the people to visit their churches. Most new residents of the neighborhood did not speak English, many had little money and all feared for their families. Even though their roots were firmly planted in the Catholic tradition, they left the Catholic church because fundamentalists spoke their language, met their needs and welcomed them.

People's needs vary from area to area, parish to parish, family to family. Consequently, it is a mistake to believe that one blueprint can address all parish needs. Only after a parish begins to appreciate peoples' physical, psychological and spiritual needs can it effectively plan to meet these needs.

Parish ministers always touch a person's heart by appealing to the individual's core or depth dimension. Everyone searches for meaning, everyone suffers and everyone needs deliverance. Since these realities underlie all evangelization efforts, it becomes easier to see how the first prerequisite for successful evangelization is welcome.

While keeping people's needs in the forefront and acknowledging the importance of welcome, parishes need to remember three presuppositions for success in parish evangelization: Evangelization is not a separate ministry; evangelization demands personal presence; evangelization is rooted in scripture and centered on sharing faith.

Not a Separate Ministry

Over-organization and specialization of ministries can lead to irresponsibility: The youth minister says, "Catechesis is not

my responsibility, it's the job of the parish school of religion";
the adult education coordinator concludes, "I'm not required to
work with senior adults. That's the job of the person hired to
minister to the aged." In a situation like this, it's not surprising
to hear people say, "Evangelization? Oh, there's a special team
to do that."

Evangelization is not a separate ministry — it is central to all
ministries. The pastor must be at the center of all organizational
efforts to further evangelization. Even if he designates someone
to oversee the practical planning aspects of it, he must insure
that all the ministries in the parish support evangelization and
incorporate elements of it into what they do.

Personal Presence

When a newly appointed pastor first offered the Sunday
liturgy in a poor, black, inner-city parish, 17 people attended.
The next day, he began to knock on doors in the neighborhood.
For six months he went house to house. His message in every
place was the same. "Hi, I'm Father Jim, the new pastor of
St. Ben's. Can I visit your home?" After spending time with
each household, he left with the words, "I appreciate your
hospitality. Now I invite you to my home. Stop and see me at
the rectory, and I'll show you where I live." Ten years later,
when Father Jim left that parish, over 700 people attended his
farewell Mass and wished him a tear-filled yet happy goodbye.

Father Jim's story reflects Jesus' way. He walked the dusty
roads of Galilee and Judea, healing people, visiting homes and
forgiving sinners. Jesus got out where the people were. So did
Father Jim. So must every evangelizer. And yet, being *around*
people is not enough. The evangelizer is challenged to be *with*
people, by being present to them. This means making people
feel important and listening to their spoken and unspoken words
and feelings.

Personal presence means people are willing to take time
with one another. Today, time is a precious commodity. When
an evangelizer gives time to another, it can have a tremendous

impact. Evangelization's success or failure often rests on the time that Christians give to others.

Centrality of Scripture and Faith Sharing

Personal presence influences evangelization's success, but more is required. The evangelist's primary function is to share faith with those who do not have it. *Evangelization in the Modern World* stresses this:

> To reveal Jesus Christ and His Gospel to those who do not know them has been, since the morning of Pentecost, the fundamental program which the Church has taken on as received from her founder (*Evangelization in the Modern World*, no. 51).

Hence, the heart of evangelization is sharing faith with those who do not believe. This implies that faith must be shared for personal presence or good works to be evangelization. Pope Paul VI stated:

> The Good News proclaimed by the witness of life sooner or later has to be proclaimed by the word of life. There is no true evangelization if the name, the teaching, the life, the promises, the kingdom and the mystery of Jesus of Nazareth, the Son of God are not proclaimed (*Evangelization in the Modern World*, no. 22).

Jesus calls every Christian to proclaim the gospel. For the mature Christian, who understands Jesus' call, evangelization is the full expression of what it means to be a Christian.

Practical Ways for a Parish to Proceed

The goal of every parish should be to help parishioners realize their part in evangelization. This includes outreach to church members, alienated Catholics and unchurched people. Any pastoral plan for parish evangelization implies two dynamics: spiritual renewal and sharing faith.

Because parishes differ in size, location, leadership, ethnic mix, parishioner mobility and needs, no one evangelization model is possible. Consequently, the organization of parish evangelization will vary according to local circumstances. At the same time, certain suggestions may help parishes develop effective evangelization. This section considers these suggestions by asking where to begin, how to proceed and what pitfalls to avoid.

Where to Begin

Jesus began his ministry by calling a few disciples and teaching them his message. Following in Jesus' footsteps, parish evangelization often begins with someone taking a leadership role and inviting several parishioners to join in an evangelization effort. The initiative for evangelization may come from the pastor, but it can also come from another parishioner, who proceeds with his approval. Without the pastor's blessing, few parish efforts, including evangelization, will have long-term success. The following steps suggest a way to begin.

1. *Designate a parish evangelization coordinator.* This person should be someone either already interested in and knowledgeable about issues of evangelization, or enthusiastic and capable of both learning about evangelization and coordinating a small group.

2. *Identify and select parishioners willing to probe the meaning of evangelization in personal and parish life.* The parishioners selected, usually four to seven, can be called the "Evangelization Team" or something similar. The purpose of this team is not primarily to do one-on-one evangelization but to discern ways that the parish itself can evangelize more effectively. In time, this team will exercise an overseeing role. It can never be viewed as solely responsible for doing evangelization in the parish.

3. *Decide on the most effective way for the team to begin.* The evangelization team needs to prepare for its ministry. This must include prayer and discernment. The biggest temptation that any newly formed group may face is to get going and produce some results. The evangelization team cannot succumb to this "heresy of action," but must take the time to ascertain how the Holy Spirit

invites this particular parish to approach evangelization. Several suggestions may help facilitate this process.

— Begin with a day of prayer or retreat.

— Center initial meetings of the group, usually weekly, on prayer, scripture and recent church teachings on evangelization. The agenda of early team meetings must include learning how Jesus and his disciples evangelized by studying the Christian scriptures, and learning what Catholic evangelization today is all about by studying contemporary church instructions on evangelization, especially Pope Paul VI's *Evangelization in the Modern World*. Without a solid biblical base, the evangelization team can get sidetracked into "the numbers game," competition or exclusivity. Without a grounding in church documents, a parish can lose its link with the larger church community. The evangelization team needs to spend considerable time, maybe as much as six months, preparing for its ministry through prayer, study and reflection.

— As the team gradually comes to appreciate more fully Jesus' evangelizing message, it constantly asks, "How can this message best be applied in our parish? What are the needs of our parishioners?"

— As the team identifies its focus, the pastor's role becomes more important. If he is not a member of the team, he should be invited to join, for the pastor is the chief parish evangelizer. If for good reasons he chooses not to join the team itself, he must be kept informed about what is happening.

How to Proceed

After the evangelization team prepares through prayer, learning and discernment, it invites the community to become an evangelizing parish. No single model exists to accomplish this, but certain points are clear.

1. *The process begins by eliciting the cooperation and leadership of the pastor.*   This is critical. The pastor's liturgical ministry of preaching, his catechetical responsibilities, and his administrative decisions to hire personnel and allocate parish funds will directly affect the success of any evangelization effort.

2. *The next step is to approach other leaders within the parish and invite them to make a commitment to evangelization.*   This includes, for example, the school principal, religious education director, parish council president, St. Vincent de Paul coordinator, liturgical director and youth minister. These people will need some education or training to understand their role in raising the parish's awareness of its evangelization responsibilities. Only after church leaders acknowledge the parish's responsibility to evangelize will evangelization succeed.

As this process occurs, a decision must be made to hire only people who are committed to evangelization for parish ministerial jobs. Likewise, only parish members who accept the parish's call to evangelize should serve in parish leadership roles such as the education committee, parish council, athletic board and finance committee. The latter committee especially must be convinced of the parish's commitment to evangelization. Otherwise, monies may be spent on misplaced parish priorities.

No new committees need be formed. An evangelizing parish does not necessarily need new structures, for it is a parish where people in existing organizations accept their responsibility to evangelize, and the entire parish recognizes its calling to proclaim God's good news.

3. *The final step involves outreach by church leaders to the broader parish population.*   In this process, the evangelization team gives support and advice to various parish committees and leaders.

The major responsibility to evangelize church members rests with the parish leaders. Several recommendations may help.

—   The pastoral team (pastor and parish leaders) formulates a practical plan for parish evangelization. Responsibility to develop this plan can be given to the evangelization team, who then submit their recommendation to parish leaders for modification or approval.

— The pastoral plan takes into account the needs of the parish, such as evangelizing youth, reconciling alienated Catholics and reaching out to unchurched people. In addition, it includes ways that various parish leaders and organizations relate and cooperate in whatever plan is established. It also suggests ways to reach the broader parish, to insure that parish members see their responsibility to evangelize. Finally, it establishes a timetable and an ongoing method of evaluation.

— A mission or spiritual renewal can initiate the wider parish process. Every parish leader is called upon to communicate the vision to his or her organization. The cooperation of parish council members, school teachers, catechists, choir members, servers, ushers, coaches and such is necessary for parish evangelization to succeed. This commitment to evangelization is ongoing, as parish personnel change. The pastor needs to reiterate the parish's evangelization commitment in homilies and in the way he encourages parishioners to extend welcome in the liturgy, meetings, parish socials and the rectory.

— As the evangelization thrust gets out to parish members through homilies, announcements, encouragement of parish leaders, youth groups and parish organizations, opportunities must be provided for parish members to learn more about scripture, church teaching and prayer. Parishioners need to see themselves as parish evangelizers in their homes, with friends, among alienated Catholics, with the unchurched, in their neighborhoods and with the civic community. A feedback system needs to be set up between parishioners and parish leaders to reach needy people and to contact potential parish members.

This process may involve some parish restructuring. The goal of the process is to call the entire parish to evangelize.

Pitfalls to Avoid

First and foremost, do not see or present evangelization as a new program. Evangelization is what Christian life is about —witness, concern and love. With this in mind, the following suggestions may help.

1. *Avoid clannishness.* After Vatican II, many parish renewal efforts deteriorated into clannishness. People active in renewal programs sometimes gave an impression of superiority. When this happened, some parishioners felt pressured to participate in renewal to be accepted by the "in crowd." Evangelization teams can fall into a similar trap of thinking they are special. When this happens, little cooperation takes place among the rest of the parish.

2. *Be open and ongoing.* Since parish evangelization is a process not a product, it must remain open and ongoing. Parishioners change and leadership changes. As this happens, accommodations need to be made.

3. *Avoid Institutionalization.* Parish evangelization cannot become one program among many, nor can it be viewed as a separate ministry. It is central to all ministry. Among other things, this means that a separate evangelization budget need not be set up. Monies allocated for evangelization can be directed through already-existing parish organizations. For example, appropriate parish ministries can budget monies for bibles, books, tapes, and funds for the poor.

4. *Do not base evangelization on money.* Evangelization's success rests on people, not money. A parish leader recently said, "We can't do much evangelization, because we are a poor parish without much money." Christians must realize they are limited creatures, and that God's Spirit evangelizes through them. They do not need expensive programs, speakers and media ads.

5. *Do not over-structure.* To accomplish its evangelization mission, parishes must establish structures to identify people's needs, organize renewal efforts and reach out to alienated Catholics or unchurched people. At the same time, room must be left for the spontaneous workings of the Holy Spirit. When too much bureaucracy exists, the structures can become more important than evangelization itself.

6. *Revolve leadership.* Every parish has certain parishioners who have been "in charge" of this or that task for years. They might work in the rectory, coordinate church functions, direct the choir or run the St. Vincent de Paul Society. Their loyalty is commendable, but their effectiveness and motivation should be questioned if they block other leaders from emerging or refuse to turn over responsibilities to others. When developing parish evangelization, establish a revolving leadership process. This can be accomplished through a three-year commitment. During the first year person A is in charge, with person B learning the job as an apprentice. In the second year, person B takes over the leadership and person C becomes the next apprentice, while person A acts as an ad-hoc consultant to person B. In the third year person B acts as a consultant to person C. This process insures both continuity of ministry and fresh leadership.

The objective of all church structures and ministries is to develop Christians who acknowledge their vocation to share faith. Evangelizers help the broader church community to see this calling. Parishes can reinvigorate their ministries through evangelization's spirit, which invites parishes to acknowledge concern for the salvation of friends and enemies and love for all people as central to Christianity.

Conclusion

It's winter now and snowflakes are falling outside the window. Soon, spring will come, and the robin I heard as I began this book on Catholic evangelization will return.

I remember the robin's song, with its echo of new life, God's love and memories of my own story. I hope I've shown that my story is every person's story, told in different times and places, and that human stories only make sense when they are faithful to God's story. Above all, I hope this book invites Christians to share Jesus' good news through their own stories.

Evangelization is every person's vocation; the parish furthers this calling as young and old, rich and poor, black, yellow, red, brown and white people join their sometimes weak and troubled hands and hearts and walk boldly into God's kingdom.